Helen Boubouli

Helen Boubouli, a foreign language teacher and entrepreneur with 30 years of experience teaching English as a second language, and a B.A in English and French from Worcester State College, is the creator of Grammar Genie.

Helen is convinced that learning can be enjoyable, creative and an interesting journey, and that grammar presented as art can motivate one to learn and equip one with valuable knowledge.

"I spent most of my teaching years writing and doing research on grammar points, and how best to present them to my students. This book is the result of thirty years of hard work that I must say I enjoyed every minute of it. Now is the time to share it with you and hope that you will benefit from it as much as I have. My students love it, and so will you."

# Table of Contents

Table of Contents _____ 2

## Grammar Genie _____ 5

## Who said Grammar was difficult? _____ 7

    http://www.boubouli.gr _____ 11

## GERUND _____ 13

    Suggest _____ 17
    Would you mind/Do you mind+ing _____ 19
    Look forward to _____ 20
    Approve of/be in favour of _____ 21
    Disapprove of/object to/oppose/ _____ 22
    be opposed to/be against/be averse to _____ 22
    It's not worth /there's no point (in)/ _____ 25
    it's no use/what's the point of _____ 25
    Be used to/be accustomed to _____ 25

## PARTICIPLES _____ 36

    Gerund vs Present participle _____ 36
    Present participle _____ 37
    Past participle _____ 39
    Perfect participle _____ 40

## GERUND/INFINITIVE _____ 41

## THE INFINITIVE _____ 50

    Expressing purpose _____ 60
    It's time _____ 61

## BARE INFINITIVE _____ 62

    Would ratner=Would sooner _____ 64
    Used to _____ 67
    Would _____ 67

## RELATIVE CLAUSES _____ 69

    Defining relative clauses _____ 69
    Non-defining relative clauses _____ 75

## LINKING WORDS (CONJUNCTIONS) _____ 77

    Subordinating Conjunctions _____ 79
        Clauses of result _____ 79
        Purpose Clauses _____ 84

| | |
|---|---|
| Time and Condition Clauses | 88 |
| Clauses of Concession or Contrast Clauses | 93 |
| Reason Clauses | 98 |
| Adding information | 100 |
| Clauses of manner | 103 |
| Conjunctions giving examples | 105 |
| Conjunctions making exceptions | 106 |
| **Coordinating Conjunctions(short conjunctions)** | **107** |
| **Correlative Conjunctions (emhasizing two things)** | **108** |

## CONDITIONALS — 110

**Progressive Verb Tenses in Conditionals** — 116
**Mixed Conditionals** — 117
**Time and condition conjunctions** — 118

## UNREAL PAST TENSES AND THE SUBJUNCTIVE — 123

**Unreal past (past subjunctive)** — 123
**Unreal Past Tenses with "Wish" = "If only"** — 124
**Unreal past tenses with: It's time** — 128
**As if/as though** — 129

## PRESENT SUBJUNCTIVE — 130

## INVERSIONS — 136

**Inverted conditional sentences** — 137

## PASSIVE VOICE — 141

**Something needs doing/Something needs to be done** — 144
**Tenses of passive voice** — 148
**Infinitives and gerunds in the passive** — 149
**Passive infinitives** — 149
**Tenses corresponding with the Infinitives** — 151

## CAUSITIVE — 152

**Have/get something done** — 152
**Have someone do something** — 153
**Get someone to do something** — 153

## PRESENT TENSES — 157

**Simple present** — 157
**Present continuous** — 164
**Present perfect** — 166
  Have gone to/have been to/have been in: — 169
  For/since: — 169

Present perfect continuous _____170

## PAST TENSES _____171
Past simple _____171
Past continuous (past progressive) _____173
Past perfect _____176
Past perfect continuous _____180
    Present perfect continuous vs past perfect continuous_____181

## FUTURE TENSES _____182
Future continuous _____187
Future perfect _____187
Future perfect continuous _____188
Special Question Tags: _____192
Agreement to affirmative sentences _____193
Agreement to negative sentences _____194
Disagreement to affirmative sentences_____194
Disagreement to negative sentences_____195

## INDIRECT SPEECH (REPORTED SPEECH) _____196
Indirect Questions (reported questions) _____203
Reporting the imperative (orders, requests, suggestions) _____205
Positive Imperative➲tell/order/advise/ask _____205

## MODAL VERBS _____211
Modal Infinitives _____219

## ADJECTIVES/ADVERBS _____223
_____227

## THE COMPARATIVE AND SUPERLATIVE OF ADJECTIVES _____228
Adjectives that have irregular comparative and superlative forms: 230

## THE COMPARATIVE AND SUPERLATIVE OF ADVERBS
_____232
Irregular adverbs: _____234
More comparisons: _____235

## THE DEFINITE ARTICLE (THE) _____237

## THE INDEFINITE ARTICLE (A/AN) _____241

## COUNTABLE NOUNS _____243

## UNCOUNTABLE NOUNS _____ 246

## QUANTIFIERS _____ 251
   **A few** vs **few** _____ 251
   **A little** vs **little** _____ 251
   **Some** _____ 251
   **Some** _____ 251
   **Any** _____ 254
   **Any** _____ 254
   **No** _____ 255
   **No** _____ 255
   **A lot of/much/many** _____ 257
   **Both/both of** _____ 258
   **Whole/all(of)** _____ 258

## Irregular Vebs _____ 260


**Learn English
with**

**Grammar Genie
by Helen Boubouli**

Copyright © 2016

by Helen Boubouli

All rights reserved. No part of this publication may be reproduced, distributed, or transmitted in any form or by any means, including photocopying, recording, or other electronic or mechanical methods, without the prior written permission of the publisher, except in the case of brief quotations embodied in critical reviews and certain other noncommercial uses permitted by copyright law.

Helen Boubouli                    **Grammar Genie**

## Who said Grammar was difficult?
### A self-study reference to grammar

A self-study reference to **Intermediate and Advanced English grammar** with clear examples and explanations aimed at students learning English as a second language, or native speakers of English wishing to learn the correct usage of the language. If you are **an English learner** and getting your message across is all you are interested in, then Grammar Genie is not for you. If you want more than just to be able to get your message across, Grammar Genie will show you the way in just 2 easy steps. The Grammar Genie makes it really easy to learn how to **speak and write correct English**.

You learn fast, easily, and without having to attend hundreds of hours of English lessons. It is designed for self-study, but it can also be used in the classroom. You learn grammar structures through lots of easy to understand examples.

**Clever and brief grammar rules, and a lot of easy to learn examples of all the grammar structures.**

**Grammar Genie says** that if you're learning English as a second language, you can learn the correct usage of grammar, both in spoken English, and in written English by following two easy steps:

Step 1 **STUDY:** You study a particular grammar structure.

Step 2 **REPEAT:** You repeat it many times to assimilate it. Learn it by heart if you can. Yes by heart. You learn one grammar structure at a time.

Repeat many times the particular grammar structure, and the examples that follow each structure to make sure you have assimilated it. **It's important that you have a lot of repetition.**

You repeat to your self the examples of the particular structure that you are studying, and you learn by listening to your self repeating something many times. After all, isn't this the way you've learned your native language by hearing something many times. In less than six months you can learn to use **the English language correctly guaranteed**.

If you are a **native speaker,** you follow the same two steps, but you will need much less time to learn a structure. In less than two months you can learn to use grammar correctly in both spoken and written English guaranteed. The way the grammar is presented is so well-thought-of that it makes learning grammar easy, fun, and most of all fast for both learners of English as a second language and native speakers too. **Grammar is presented in the most innovative way ever.**

Learning English can be fun, and you can learn it on your own without having to attend classes.

**Grammar Genie** addresses all those who want to save time and money. My students love it, and so will you. They learn three structures a week on their own at home, and we spend the time in class doing oral work, listening, and drilling. Instead of spending endless hours talking about grammar, we use the grammar structures that we have studied in drilling and speaking in the classroom. You learn fast, yes, really fast. Whoever said that grammar is difficult should definitely reconsider.

Try learning with the Grammar Genie.

If you are an English teacher, Grammar Genie does all the work for you.

If you are an **English teacher,** you can use Grammar Genie as reference to teach grammar. It's really easy to teach, and your students learn easily.

Grammar is a resource which enables you to get your message across correctly.

The aim of Grammar Genie is to discourage students and teachers from seeing grammar as a set of rules, to help them to develop a richer understanding of the relationship between language and context, and to view grammar as a resource for getting their message across using the correct language.

Although Grammar Genie is designed for self-study, it can also be used as reference in the classroom. It's a unique grammar reference for ESL/EFL teachers, and for ESL/EFL students from Intermediate to Advanced levels.

Making grammar mistakes is attributed to not knowing the correct usage of the language. The Grammar Genie shows you how to improve both your speaking and writing skills easily, painlessly, and effortlessly. The Grammar Genie is a pioneer in the way grammar is presented.

Don't wait. Learn English with this unique and most clever method ever, now.

**http://www.boubouli.gr**
elena@masterlingua.gr

*This book is dedicated to the memory of my father, Dimitrios Bouboulis. May he rest in peace.
To my mother, who I owe so much to,*

*my students and family, my daughters, my husband, my sister and my niece, each of whom has a special place in my heart.*

*With special gratitude to Romy and Dimitra, the best daughters I could ever imagine
You have been a gift to me. I am so privileged to have you.*

# GERUND

## Forms of the gerund

We form the gerund by adding **ing** to the verb:

I don't like play**ing** cards.

In passive voice it is formed with **being +past participle**:

I dislike **being attacked.**

We use **perfect gerund** both in active voice and passive voice to refer to the past:

The thief denied **having stolen** the money. (Active voice)
I appreciate **having been informed** promptly. (Passive voice)
I apologise for **having come** late.

|  | **Active Voice** | **Passive voice** |
|---|---|---|
| **Present gerund:** | attacking | being attacked |
| **Perfect gerund:** | having attacked | having been attacked |

Instead of using **perfect gerund** we can use **present gerund** with no change in meaning:

Tom denied **attacking** me. ➲Active present gerund
        or
Tom denied **having attacked** me. ➲Active perfect gerund

Ann reported **being attacked.** ➲Passive present gerund
        or
Ann reported **having been attacked.** ➲Passive perfect gerund

## Use of the gerund

**We use a gerund**

**as the subject of a sentence:**

**Cycling** helps me keep fit.

> We use **not+gerund** to form a negative gerund:
>
> **Not talking** to me won't help you solve your problem.

**as the object of a sentence:**

I really enjoy **writing.**

I don't enjoy **writing.**

**after all prepositions:**

He left **without saying** goodbye.

He succeeded **by trying** hard.

**after possessive adjectives or object pronouns:**

I look forward to **his/him coming.**

I suggest **your/you working** a little harder for this exam.

**after genitive case:**

John denied **Helen's cheating** in the test.

**after nouns:**

Did you forget your **mother** telling you not to go outside?

**after adjectives** that are usually **followed by a preposition:**

| | | |
|---|---|---|
| be against | be averse to | be accustomed to |
| be addicted to | be afraid of | be anxious about |
| be bored of | be capable of | be committed to |
| be concerned about | be content with | be dedicated to |
| be devoted to | be disappointed with | be discouraged by/from |
| be excited about | be famous for | be frightened of |
| be guilty of | be happy about | be interested in |
| be involved in | be known for | be opposed to |
| be obsessed with | be proud of | be remembered for |
| be responsible for | be scared of | be terrified of |
| be tired from/ of | be worried about etc. | |

My students **are busy studying** for their exams.

**We're tired of doing** the same things every single day.

**I'm excited about** going to London.

**She's interested in** learning Chinese.

**I'm good at** playing the piano.

## after certain verbs:

| | | |
|---|---|---|
| anticipate | **appreciate** | avoid |
| appreciate | **avoid** | celebrate |
| comprehend | **contemplate** | defer |
| confess (to) | **consider** | contemplate |
| deny | **delay** | detest |
| deny | **detest** | dread |
| dislike | **discuss** | enjoy |
| dislike | **doubt** | enjoy |
| entail | **envisage** | escape |
| escape, | **admit (to)** | anticipate |
| evade | excuse | **Face** |
| fancy | **favour** | feel like |
| finish | **forgive** | *forget (if it refers to the past) |
| *hate (if it refers to the past) | **imagine** | foresee |
| involve | **like** | loath |
| keep | **miss** | overlook |
| mention | **mean** | mind |
| mind | **understand** | waste time/money |
| need | **demand** | recollect |
| pardon | **postpone** | practice |
| propose | **prohibit** | quit |
| recommend | **recall** | *regret (if it refers to the past) |
| relish | ***remember (if it refers to the past)** | renounce |
| repent | **require** | resent |
| require | **report** | insist |
| resist | **resume** | resume |
| risk | ***stop (if it refers to the past)** | suggest |
| suffer | **suggest** | miss |
| tolerate | | |

> *Regret, stop, remember, **forget+ing** for **past reference**
> Regret, stop, remember, **forget+full infinitive** for **present reference** or **future reference**

I regret **telling** you the truth. (=I wish I hadn't told you the truth.)

I regret **to tell** you that your cat was run over by a car. (=I'm sorry to tell you that your cat was run over by a car.)

They stopped **talking** when I entered the room (=They were talking, and they stopped as soon as I entered the room.)

While I was walking home I ran into an old friend and **I stopped to talk** to him.
(=I stopped walking in order to talk to my friend.)

I remember **locking** the door. (=I locked the door.)

Remember **to lock** the door when you leave the house. (=Don't forget to lock the door when you leave.)

I **forgot to invite** Nina to our party. (=I didn't invite Nina to the party.)

I think you **forgot inviting** Nina to the party because I heard you invite her.
(=You invited Nina but you forgot that you invited her.)

> **suggest**+ing ➲ **We use a gerund when we have one subject:**

I suggest **going** to the movies.
(=I suggest that we should go to the movies.)

He suggested **babysitting** for us, so we could go out for a change.
(=he offered to babysit for us, so we could go out for a change.)

**Note:** When there is a change of subject we use **that clause + the bare infinitive(subjunctive):**

**Suggest(that) someone (should) do sth**⮕The bare infinitive is used with or without "should".
**(Suggest(that)+subject pronoun+ (should)+bare infinitive)**

✓I suggest (that) he (should) see a doctor.

**(Although simple past can also be used when the introductory verb (suggest) is in the past, the infinitive or the should construction is recommended)**

✓I suggested( **that) he see/saw** a doctor.

✓I suggested( that ) he ( should) see a doctor.

✗I suggest( that) he saw a doctor.**(Simple past cannot be used when the introductory verb "suggest" is not in the past.**

**(Simple present is also possible when the introductory verb (suggest) is in the present but the infinitive or the should construction is recommended.)**

✓I suggest **that he sees** a doctor

✓I suggest **that he see** a doctor

✓I suggest **that he should see** a doctor

✗I suggested that he ~~sees~~ a doctor. **(simple present cannot be used when "suggest"is not in the present.**

✓I suggested( **that) he see/saw** a doctor.

## Would you mind/Do you mind+ing

Would you mind **doing** sth?
Would you mind if I, he, she, we, they **did** sth **(unreal past for the present)**
Do you mind **doing** sth
Do you mind if I, he, she, we, they **do** sth
**Would you mind opening the window?(= Could you please open the window?)**

☑**Would you mind if I, she, we, they opened the window? (=Could I open the window? )**(unreal past for the present)

☒**Would you mind if I, she, we, they open the window?**

☑ **Do you mind opening the window?(= Can you open the window?)**

☑ **Do you mind if I, she, we, they open the window? (= Can I open the window?)**

### verb+preposition+ing

| | |
|---|---|
| **approve of** | I **don't approve of** smoking in public places. |
| **decide against** | I **decided against** trying to influence you. |
| **disapprove of** | I **disapprove of** underpaying immigrants. |
| **dream about/of** | I'm **dreaming about** going away with you. |
| **end up** | He **ended up** staying a bachelor. |
| **feel like** | I **feel like** taking the day off. |
| **look forward to** | We **look forward to** seeing you. |
| **object to** | I **object to** working over-time. |
| **succeed in** | **Helen succeeded in getting** the proficiency. |
| **think about/of** | I'm **thinking about** coming to see you this weekend. |

**with most of the above verbs the following construction is also possible:**
**verb+ preposition+(possessive adjective/object pronoun/ proper noun)+ing**
**verb+preposition+(my/your/his/her/our/their/me/you/ him/her/their/our/**

| | |
|---|---|
| **look forward to** | doing **something** **my/your/his/her/our/their me/you/him/her/their/our Ann doing** something **(my/your/his/her/our/their me/you/him/her/their/our) doing something** |

look forward to+**ing**
 **look forward to**+possessive adjective/object pronoun +ing
look forward to +noun

**I dream about your/you/ getting** your degree.

**I look forward to his/John coming** with us.

**I disapprove of your smoking.**

**It's formal when simple present is used:**
We **look forward to** seeing you.

**It's informal when present continuous is used:**
The students **are looking forward to** going on the field trip.

➲

**I'm looking forward to** seeing you. ➲ informal

I **look forward to** hearing from you. ➲ formal

I **look forward to** your prompt reply.

I'm **looking forward to** Christmas.

## Approve of/be in favour of

| approve of/be in favour of | (my/your/his/her/their/our me/you/him/her/us/them / Jim's) | doing something |
|---|---|---|
| approve of/be in favour of | | something |

My parents **approve of** my working hard for school.

**I approve of** his refusing to testify in court.

**I'm in favour** of our rehearsing everyday after school for the play.

All non-smokers **are in favour of** the law against smoking in public places.

Most parents **don't approve of** their kids going out every night.

Most people **approve of** the government enforcing stricter laws to combat crime.

## Disapprove of/object to/oppose/ be opposed to/be against/be averse to

| disapprove of<br>object to<br>be opposed to | ( my /your/<br>his/her/their/our<br>me/you<br>/him/her/us/them<br>Jim's ) | doing something |
|---|---|---|
| oppose<br>be against<br>be averse to | | something. |

All of us here **are against** drugs.

The president of this company **disapproves of/objects to** our coming in late for work.

Our teacher **disapproves of/objects to** our speaking Greek in class.

**I am opposed to/ averse to** smoking in public places.

I **disapprove of** my kids misbehaving in class.

Most parents **disapprove of/object to their kids staying** out late.

after verb + object pronoun(me,you,him,her,it,us,them) /proper noun(George etc) + preposition:

| **thank someone for doing something** | prevent someone from doing something |
|---|---|
| **forgive someone for doing something** | warn someone against doing something |
| **suspect someone of doing something** | accuse someone of doing something |
| **stop someone from doing something** | discourage someone from doing something |
| **lure someone into doing something** | entice someone into doing something |
| **talk someone into doing something** | |

He **discouraged me from trying** to convince him.

He **thanked me for helping** him.

I **warned Jim against trusting** his partner.

I will never **forgive you for lying/having lied** to me.

after certain expressions used to talk about certain sports and activities that you engage in:

| | | |
|---|---|---|
| | **jogging** | **He goes jogging** for half an hour every day. |
| | **shopping** | I only **go shopping** for clothes during sales |
| | **sightseeing** | When I travel abroad I like **to go sightseeing** more than anything else. |
| **go(come)+** | **mountaineering** | **Mountaineering** is the activity of climbing mountains. |
| | **fishing** | Bill likes **to go fishing** once in a while. |
| | **sailing** | **Going sailing** in the summer is Ruth's hobby. |
| | **clubbing** | Every now and then Tonia **goes clubbing** with her friends. |
| | **swimming** | How often does Veronica **go swimming?** |

## waste/spend time, money + ing

Andrew **wastes all his money buying** useless gadgets.

Jim **spends a lot of time reading** books.

Most children in Greece **spend most of their youth studying**.

## waste of time, money+ing

**It's a waste of time watching** television.

**It's a waste of money buying** clothes that you'll probably never wear.

| | | |
|---|---|---|
| have difficulty(in) | | **I have difficulty in understanding** her accent. |
| have a difficult time | | With all the noice outside, **the students are having a difficult time hearing** the teacher. |
| have a hard time | **doing something** | **I have a hard time making** ends meet. |
| have trouble | | I **have trouble convincing** my parents to let me go on the school trip. |

| | | |
|---|---|---|
| **find something difficult** | | I **find it difficult to understand** her accent. |
| find something hard | **to do** | Mary **finds it hard to cope** with her teen age daughter. |

## It's not worth /there's no point (in)/ it's no use/what's the point of

| | | |
|---|---|---|
| it's not worth | | It's not worth talking to him. He won't listen whatever you say |
| there's no point (in) | | **There's no point (in) trying** to console him. He's inconsolable. |
| it's no use | +ing | **It's no use trying** to console him. He's inconsolable. |
| it's no good | | **It's no good trying** to console him. He's inconsolable. |
| what's the point of | | **What's the point of** trying to console him? He's inconsolable. |

### something needs doing/something needs to be done

My hair **needs trimming.**

My hair **needs to be trimmed.**

The house **needs doing up**.

The house **needs to be done up.**

## Be used to/be accustomed to

**be used to/be accustomed to+ing ⮕ present habit**
**be used to/ be accustomed to+ noun**

I'm **used to drinking** tea.

I'm **used to tea.**

I'm **accustomed to eating** healthy food.

I'm **accustomed to healthy food.**

**get used / get accustomed to + ing** ➲ **try to aquire the habit of doing something or become used to something**
**get used / get accustomed to + noun**

**I'm trying to get used to waking up early.**
(=I'm not used to waking up early, but I'm trying to acquire the habit of waking up early.)

**I can't get used to the cold weather in America.**
(=I can't become accustomed to the cold weather.)

**I got used to my new English teacher.**
(=I wasn't used to my new English teacher in the beginning but now I am.)

vs

**used to + bare infinitive (past habits/facts/states.)**
**( See page 65-67 for more on "used to")**

When I was a little girl **I used to play** with dolls (past habit) (I don't play with dolls anymore.)

I **used to like** Sports. (state) (I don't like Sports anymore.)

George **used to be** a careless driver. (fact) (He's not a careless driver anymore.)

**to express purpose:**

**with a view to doing something/ with the aim of doing somehing/with the intention of doing something/with the hope of doing something(positive)**

He went to bed early **with a view to getting** some sleep.

He left early **with the aim of being** on time for the interview

**to avoid doing/ for fear of doing(NEGATIVE)**

He rushed **to avoid missing** the bus.

He rushed **for fear of missing** the bus.

>**but**

**for fear I/you/he might do sth (when there is a change of subject)**

He rushed **for fear he might miss** the bus.

**to add information:**

**as well as, apart from, besides, except (for), let alone, in addition**

Alex is studying Chinese **as well as studying** English.

**As well as studying** Chinese, Alex is studying English.

I didn't do anything else this summer **apart from/except for lying** on the beach all day long.

I hate reading in general on my vacation **let alone having** to study for summer classes.

**(See page 102 for more on clauses of adding information.)**

**with some expressions:**

**be busy doing something**

I'm going to be **busy studying** for my exams all week.

### can't bear/can't stand, can't help, have fun/a good time

**I can't bear having** to work on weekends.

**I can't help eating** sweets.

**I had so much fun dancing** all evening.

**We had such a good time horse riding** this week end.

### what do you say to

**What do you say to going** away for the weekend?
(=How would you like to go away for the weekend?)

### when it comes to

**When it comes to clubbing** most teenagers are always willing.
(=Most teenagers never say no to clubbing.)

### on+gerund

**On seeing Steve enter the house, Jane sighed with relief.**
(=When Jane saw Steve enter the house, she sighed with relief.)

Helen Boubouli Grammar Genie

The following are just some of the most common verbs, adjectives, nouns and expressions listed in groups, followed by the same preposition(for) +ing

| | | |
|---|---|---|
| account for | **admire someone for** | arrest someone for |
| apologize (to someone) for | **be in the mood for (feel like doing something)** | be famous for |
| be renowned for | **be responsible for** | be sorry for (past reference) |
| bear someone a grudge for | **have/hold a grudge against someone for** | harbor a grudge against sm for |
| bear someone no grudge for | **have/hold no grudge against someone for** | harbour no grudge against sm for |
| blame someone for | **care for (like)** | compensate for |
| condemn someone for | **commend someone for (praise)** | criticize someone for |
| despise someone for | **find an excuse for** | forgive someone for |
| get revenge on someone for | **get one's back on someone** | forgive someone for |
| credit someone for | **have a flair for** | have a talent for |
| have a gift for | **make allowances for (be lenient)** | make up for |
| pardon someone for | **praise someone for** | prosecute someone for |
| punish someone for | **rebuke someone for** | reprimand someone for |
| reproach someone for (speak severely to someone) | **reward someone for** | scold someone for |
| suffer for | **sue someone for** | take revenge on someone for |
| tell someone off for (scold) | **thank someone for** | |

The judge **made allowances for his being** a minor and gave him a light sentence.

Teachers should always **commend their students for trying** hard.

Verbs, adjectives and nouns followed by "of"+gerund:

| | | |
|---|---|---|
| accuse someone of | **acquit someone of** | approve of |
| be afraid of | **be ashamed of** | be apprehensive of |
| be capable of | **be confident of** | be doubtful of |
| be uncomfortable about | **be fearful of** | be fond of |
| be frightened of | **be guilty of** | be horrified of |
| be in flavor of | **be in the habit of doing something** | have the habit of doing something |
| be on the point of | **be on the verge of** | be proud of |
| be scared of | **be terrified of** | be thinking of |
| be wary of | **be worthy of** | boast of |
| complain of/about | **consist of** | deprive someone of |
| disapprove of | **dream of** | have no intention of |
| have enough of | **make no secret of** | make no mention of |
| suspect someone of | the anxiety of | |
| the advantage of | the chance of | the danger of |
| the feeling of | the drawback of | the likelihood of |
| the risk of | the satisfaction of | be sick of |
| the prospect of | the point of | |

## Verbs, adjectives and nouns followed by "about" + gerund:

| be angry about | **be anxious about** | boast about |
|---|---|---|
| bother about | **be concerned about** | dream about/of |
| be enthusiastic about | **be excited about** | be lazy about |
| make a fuss about | **make a scene about** | be optimistic about |
| be pessimistic about | **be serious about** | be sensitive about |
| have no scruples about | **be sorry about** | speak about |
| talk about(of) | **think about/of** | be unhappy about |
| be upset about | **be uneasy about** | |

## Verbs, predicative adjectives and nouns followed by "in"+gerund:

| be absorbed in | **believe in** | co-operate in |
|---|---|---|
| be involved in | **be justified in** | participate in |
| be pessimistic in(about) | **be prompt in** | be quick in |
| collaborate in | **have(no) difficulty in** | be engrossed in |
| have (no) trouble in | **be interested in** | be implicated in |
| have no hesitation in | **indulge in** | lose no time in |
| result in | **specialize in** | succeed in |
| take part in | **take pride in** | take pleasure in |
| take the initiative in | | |

A lot of people **have difficulty in reading** most doctors' prescriptions.

**You should never have taken the initiative in informing** my parents about my marital problems.

**I take pleasure in reading** myself to sleep.

**Indulging in drinking and smoking** can be hazardous to your health.

Verbs, predicative adjectives and nouns followed by "at"+gerund:

| aim at | **be angry at** | be annoyed at |
|---|---|---|
| be clever at | **draw the line at** | frown at |
| be good/bad at | **have a go/shot at** | laugh at |
| smile at | **be an expert at** | |

Verbs, predicative adjectives and nouns followed by "into"+gerund:

| **blackmail someone into** | bully someone into | **coerce someone into** |
|---|---|---|
| **delude someone into** | force someone into | **lure someone into** |
| **mislead someone into** | persuade someone into (formal) | **talk someone into** (informal) |
| **trick someone into** | talk someone out of (dissuade sm from ) | entice sm into |

*Note:* Both **"persuade sm into doing sth"** (formal) and **"persuade sm to do sth"** are correct

An eleven-year-old kid **bullied a class mate of his into giving him** his pocket money.

You lied to me and **tricked me into coming** with you.

You will never **talk me into lying** to my best friend.(=You will never persuade me to lie)

I tried to **talk him out of doing** something that he doesn't believe in.

## Verbs followed by "from"+ing

| abstain from | get (no) benefit from | restrain someone from |
|---|---|---|
| ban someone from | get (no) pleasure from | stop someone from |
| deduce /infer something from | hinder someone from | rescue someone from |
| deter someone from | prevent someone from | stop someone from |
| discourage someone from | protect someone from | suffer from |
| dissuade someone from | refrain someone from | get (no) satisfaction from |
| exempt someone from | save someone from | |

**Abstain/refrain from smoking and drinking** if you wish to be healthy.

**He was exempted from serving** in the army due to his ill health.

## Verbs and predicative adjectives followed by "on"+gerund:

| be bent on | be keen on | compliment someone on |
|---|---|---|
| concentrate on focus one's attention on | count on insist on | depend on pride oneself on |
| have one's heart set on | spend money on | sympathize with someone on |
| be an authority on (expert in) | | |

**I pride my self on** my cooking.(=**I take pride in** my cooking)

**I pride my self on being** fluent in four languages.(=**I take pride in** being fluent in four languages)

Verbs and adjectives followed by "to" +gerund or "to" +noun:

| adapt to | adjust to | allude to |
|---|---|---|
| attribute something to | ascribe something to | be accustomed to |
| be addicted to | be averse to | be close to |
| be committed to | be equivalent to | be impervious to |
| be opposed to | come round to | contribute to |
| bring someone round to(persuade) | | |
| confess to | dedicate to | devote oneself to |
| expose oneself to | feel up to | get accustomed to |
| get/become acclimatized to | get round o | get used to |
| look forward to | make allusion to(refer to) | object to |
| plead guilty to | put someone up to | refer to |
| resign oneself to | resort to | stoop to |
| be up to(feel like) | be used to | succumb to |

I will not **succumb to** your wishes under any circumstances.

His ill **health is attributed to** his working hard.

I'm trying to **bring her round to** joining us for dinner.

I'm not **up to** coming.

**Who put you up to** lying to us.

Verbs and adjectives followed by "with"+gerund or noun:

be obsessed with
hang around/out with

Most teenagers like to **hang around with their peers**.

Verbs and adjectives followed by"against"+gerund or noun:

| **warn someone against** | vote against | **react against** |
|---|---|---|
| **advise someone against/on** | conspire against | **be prejudiced against** |

**I warned you against hanging around/out** with someone who has no respect for your needs.

**Being prejudiced against people** who are different than you is being ignorant.

# PARTICIPLES
## Gerund vs Present participle
### Gerund

The structure of a present participle and a gerund is the same-ing, while there is a difference in the way they are used. If an **-ing** is **used as a noun it is a gerund,** if it is **used as an adjective, a verb or a modifier (modifying a noun) it is a participle**(-ing or -ed if regular):

**A gerund or a perfect gerund is used:**

**as a subject of a sentence**

**Listening** to music is fun.⮞gerund

**Watching** TV is a waste of time.

**Preparing** for the proficiency involves working hard.

**Having been released** from the hospital, I went straight to work.⮞perfect gerund

(=When I was released from the hospital, I went straight to work.)

**as an object of a sentence**

Everybody likes **listening** to music.

**preceded by a possessive adjective**

Forgive **my coming** late.

I don't recommend **your** staying at that hotel.

**preceded by genitive case** (John's book, Helen's mother, the children's toys)

**The students'** arriving late for class led to its cancellation.

Helen's **passing** her final exams with an 'A' was no surprise to me.

## Present participle

**Structure:** -ing

**The active present participle-ing is used:**

**as a verb** to replace continuous tenses and continuous infinitives after "if, when, while, though"

He was studying **while listening** to music.
(=He was studying **while** he was listening to music.)

**to replace a clause containing as, since, because**

Continuously **arriving** late, he was fired.
(=He was fired **because** he continuously arrived late.)

**Not having to go** to class tomorrow, he will catch up on his studying.
(=**Since he doesn't have to go** to class tomorrow, he will catch up on his studying.)

**Being** my birthday, I decided to throw a party for my friends.
(=**Since it was** my birthday, I decided to throw a party for my friends.)

**as an adjective used to talk about how something has influenced somebody: boring, interesting, disappointing, exciting, surprising**

I find science fiction books **interesting.**

What a **boring** day this is!

A **talking** parrot.

A **washing** machine.

**as a verb to replace relative clauses**

The view from the house **overlooking** the park is breathtaking.
(=The view from the house **which is overlooking** the park is breathtaking.)

The boy **running** down the street is my grandson.
(=The boy **who is running** down the street is my grandson)

**to replace subject and verb in the main clause of subject clause if the subject is the same**

He ran to catch the bus **holding** two heavy suitcases.

**Holding** two heavy suitcases, he ran to catch the bus.

(=**He** ran to catch the bus while **he** was holding two heavy suitcases.)


While **talking** on the phone, he was having lunch.

(=While **she** was talking on the phone, s**he** was having lunch.)


If **jogging**, you must wear athletic shoes.

(=If **you** are jogging, **you** must wear athletic shoes.)


**The negative structure of a present active participle is** "not+ing":

**Not having** anything to do he caught up with some sleep.

## Past participle

**Structure:** If the verb is regular the structure is **-ed,** Irregular verbs have different forms.

**Use:** A past participle is used:

**like relative clauses to replace subject and verb when the meaning is passive**

A house, **built** in Victorian style, is usually more extravagant than a modern home.
(=A house, **which is built** in Victorian style, is usually more extravagant than a modern style home)

The woman **mugged** down the street is my grand mother.
(=The woman **who was mugged** down the street is my grand mother.)

**as an adjective or a modifier (modifying a noun) before a noun**

An **interested** student.
**Developed** countries.
**Broken** dishes.
**Grown** children.

# Perfect participle

**Structure:** Active perfect participle⇒having + past participle **(having done)**
Passive perfect participle⇒having been +past **participle (having been done)**

**Use:** A perfect participle is used to show that an action took place before another past action

**Active perfect participle:**
**Having arrived** late at the airport, I missed my flight.
(=Because I arrived late at the airport, I missed my flight.)

**Passive perfect participle:**
**Having been released** from the hospital, I went straight to work.
(=When I was released from the hospital, I went straight to work.)

Note: You can sometimes use the present participle to replace the perfect participle with no change in meaning:

After **having finished** his work, he turned in.(perfect participle)
(=After he finished his work, he turned in.)
                              or
After **finishing** his work, he turned in. (present participle)
(=After he finished his work, he turned in.)

## GERUND/INFINITIVE

The **gerund or the infinitive** is used **after the following verbs** with no change in meaning:

| attempt   | cease      | neglect |
|-----------|------------|---------|
| begin     | like       | love    |
| can't bear| can't stand| start   |
| continue  | intend     | hate    |
| prefer    | propose    |         |

I like **learning/to learn** languages.

I can't bear **waking up/ to wake up** very early in the morning.

We use **like + gerund** when we want to say that we enjoy doing something in general:

I **like watching** television.

I **like sleeping.**

**We use like +full infinitive** to refer to a specific time or when we want to say that we choose to do something because we consider it right even though we don't enjoy it:

**I like to clean** my house on Sundays.
(It's not something that I enjoy doing, but it's what I have to do.)

We use the **infinitive after "only" to express annoyance:**

I went early for the interview **only** to find out that someone else was given the job.

We only use **an infinitive** after the **verbs begin, start, continue,** if they are in a continuous form:

**I'm starting to get** tired.
                    **but**

**I started** to **get/getting** tired.


**Needs+ infinitive** vs **needs+ing** with no change in meaning:

My hair **needs cutting**. (gerund)

My hair **needs to be cut**. (passive infinitive)


**The infinitive is used** when the verbs begin, start, continue are followed by the verbs understand, know, realize :

**I started to realize** what was happening when it was too late to do anything about it.

**Verbs and Adjectives +Infinitive or Gerund** with a change of meaning:

| remember | forget | stop |
|---|---|---|
| **go** | regret | **try** |
| **mean** | keen | **propose** |
| **want** | sorry | **hate** |
| **dread** | be keen | **be interested** |

**Remember +ing ➲ refers to a past action** you bring back to memory:

I **remember locking** the door before I left the house.(= I locked the door before I left the house.)

You came home really drunk last night. Do you **remember being sick** and **throwing up.**(=You were sick and you threw up.)

**Remember +full infinitive➲ refers to a present or future action** you plan to do or not to do:

Please **remember to lock the door** when you leave the office.(=You should not forget to lock the door.)

Will you **remember to call** me as soon as your plane lands?(= Don't forget to call me as soon as your plane lands.)

**Forget +ing➲** refers to a **past action:**

I received the same e-mail twice. **She must have forgotten sending** it to me.(=She sent me the e-mail and she forgot that she sent it to me.)

**I forgot your telling me** to take the day off today.
(=You told me to take the day off today, but I forgot it.)

**Forget+ full infinitive➲** refers to a **present or future** action you forget or not forget to do:

If you **forget to wake me up** tomorrow morning, I'll miss the bus. (=Wake me up in the morning, or I'll miss the bus.)

We will be robbed if **I forget to lock** the door again.
(=I should not forget to lock the door.)

**Stop+ing ⇒ finish doing something:**

At 2 o'clock in the morning I decided to **stop studying**.
(=I didn't study any more after 2 o'clock...)

**Stop talking** so that we can check the grammar exercises.
(=Don't talk any more.)

**Stop+ full infinitive ⇒ stop something in order to do sth else:**

At 2 o'clock in the morning I **stopped to go** to sleep.
(=I stopped what I was doing in order to go to sleep.)

**We stopped to check** the exercises.
(=We stopped what we were doing in order to check the exercises.)

**Go on+ing ⇒ continue doing what you were doing:**

Please **go on talking**.
(=Don't stop talking.)

**Go on+ full infinitive ⇒ stop what you were doing in order to do sth else:**

Close your books **and go on to write** a composition.
(=Stop whatever you were doing in order to write your composition.)

**Regret +ing ⇒ have doubts about a past action:**

I **regret telling** you the truth.
(=I wish I had not told you the truth.)

I **regret going** on that trip. I had a terrible time.
(=I wish I hadn't gone on that trip.)

**Regret +infinitive ⊃ be sorry about something that you have to do in the PRESENT/FUTURE:**

**I regret to tell you** that your credit card has expired.
(=I'm sorry to have to tell you that your credit card has expired.)

**I regret to inform you** that your thesis is overdue.
(=I'm sorry to tell you this.)

**Try+ing ⊃ do sth as an experiment to see what will happen:**

**I tried adding** some curry to the spaghetti sauce and it came out really good.
**Try cutting down on** carbs if you want to lose weight.

**Try +full infinitive ⊃ make an effort to do** something (try to do something that might be difficult):

**I tried to talk** to her but she wouldn't listen.

**Try to learn** infinitives and gerunds by doing a lot of exercises.

My teacher **tried to encourage me** to have more confidence in myself.

**Mean +ing ⊃ involve/entail/ require:**

Doing the proficiency **means studying** really hard.

I got a new job, and it's very demanding. It **means getting up** very early in the morning.

### Mean+full infinitive ⮕ intend/ plan:

I'm sorry, **I didn't mean to hide** the truth from you.
(=I didn't intend to hide the truth from you.)

**I meant to come** earlier, but I was delayed at work.
(=I intended to come earlier.)

### Keen on/interested in+ing ⮕ interested in sth in general:

**I'm keen on/interested in learning** foreign languages.

**I'm keen on/interested in working out.**

### Keen /interested+full infinitive ⮕ interested in sth specific:

**I'm keen/ interested to learn** how to speak Chinese.

**I'm keen/ interested to hear** what he has to say about it.

### Propose +ing ⮕ suggest:

**I propose your taking a** few days off work because you definitely need to rest.

**(=I suggest your taking a** few days off work because you definitely need to rest.)

### Propose +full infinitive ⮕ intend:

**I propose to tell her** what happened the minute I see her.
**(=I intend to tell her** what happened the minute I see her.)

### Want +ing ⮕ need/ require:

My house **wants/needs redecorating**.

### Want +full infinitive ⮕ have the need to do sth:

**I want to apologise** for keeping this from you.

**Sorry +full infinitive ⇒ regret sth/ be in the difficult position to say sth:**

**I'm sorry to tell you** that your application for the post has been turned down.

**Sorry for +ing ⇒ apologise for sth:**

**I'm so sorry for being** late.(=She apologized for being late.)

**Hate +ing ⇒ feel bad about doing sth/ despise/ not like at all:**

**I hate working** night shifts.

**I hate lying** to my parents.

**Hate +full infinitive ⇒ feel bad about what one has to do:**

**I hate to tell you** this, but your letter of application has been rejected.

**I hate to borrow** money from you, but I promise to pay you back as soon as I get payed.

**Dread+ full infinitive ⇒ feel really anxious/worried about something:**

**I dread to think about** what might happen when our parents come home and see this mess.

**Dread+gerund ⇒ not like at all, despise/ be afraid of:**

**I dread waking up** at 5: 00 o'clock in the morning to go to work.

The bare infinitive or gerund after some verbs especially verbs of perception with a change of meaning:

| feel | hear | listen to |
|---|---|---|
| **look at** | notice | **observe** |
| **perceive** | see | **smell** |
| **watch** | | |

The **bare infinitive** for a complete action, **-ing** for part of an action or an action in progress:

I **saw you take** my money from my brief case.(= I saw the whole action.)

I **saw you taking** my money from my brief case.(=I saw part of the action)

I **heard you sing** the song that I wrote for you the other day and I was captivated.
(= I heard the song from the beginning to the end.)

I **heard you singing** the song that I wrote for you the other day and I was captivated. (=You were singing when I came and I heard part of the song.)

### Prefer

| | |
|---|---|
| **prefer doing** something **to doing** something else ☞ | It refers to something in general. |
| **prefer doing** something **rather than doing** something else ☞ | |
| **prefer to do** something **rather than (to) do** something else ☞ | |
| **would prefer to do** something **than to do** something else ☞ | It refers to something specific. |
| **would rather do** something **than do** something else ☞ | |

48

I **prefer going** to the cinema **to** watching television .

I **prefer going** out **rather than staying** home.

I **prefer to do** sports **rather than (to) go** to a gym.

I **would prefer to watch** television tonight **rather than (to) go** to the cinema.

I **would rather watch** television tonight **than go** to the cinema.

**Also: It would have been better if+ past perfect⮕refers to the past**

**It would have been better if you had joined us last night.**

## THE INFINITIVE
### Forms of the infinitive

|  | Active voice | Passive voice |
|---|---|---|
| Present infinitive: | **(to) inform** | **(to) be informed** |
| Present continuous Infinitive: | **(to) be informing** | ------------------------------ |
| Perfect infinitive: | **(to) have informed** | **(to) have been informed** |
| Perfect continuous infinitive: | **(to) have been informing** | ------------------------------ |

**Active voice**      **passive voice**

You must not **reveal** this to anyone. It must not **be revealed** to anyone.
The kids must **be sleeping.**-------------------------------------------
You should **have informed** me. I should **have been informed.**

**Have you been working** all day? ------------------------------------

## FULL INFINITIVE
## Use of the infinitive

**The full infinitive** is used with **"it"** as the subject of a sentence**(it's important, it's necessary:)**

Is it necessary **to attend** this lecture?

It is important **to understand** what you have to do in case of emergency.

**It** is a wise decision **to save your** money.

**A gerund** is often used as the subject of a sentence:

**Saving** your money is a wise decision

**An infinitive** is also used but it's less common than the **it+ infinitive construction:**

**To save your** money is a wise decision.

**It is** a wise decision **to save** your money.


The **full infinitive** is used after**:**

**the following verbs**

| afford | agree | appear |
|---|---|---|
| arrange | beg | bother |
| care(want) | choose | consent |
| claim | demand | decide |
| expect | fail | help |
| attempt | decide | encourage |
| endeavor | forbid | get |
| happen | hasten | hurry |
| hesitate | hope | intend |
| invite | learn | long |
| manage | neglect | offer |
| omit | pretend | plan |

| prepare    | promise     | refuse      |
|------------|-------------|-------------|
| remind     | seem        | shudder     |
| swear      | tend        | threaten    |
| tell       | undertake   | volunteer   |
| vow        | want        | wish(want)  |
| would hate | would like  | would love  |
| yearn      | prefer, etc |             |

**He seemed to be** sick.

**He threatened to kill me.**

My professors **encouraged me to try** harder.

Please **help me (to)understand** this problem.

**I shudder to think** what will happen if there is a tsunami here in Greece.

*NOTES* :He appears,seems,claims +full infinitive
vs
It appears/it seems+ that clause

Helen seems **to be** sick. (present infinitive)
**It seems that Helen** is sick.

Romy appears **to have left** early. (perfect infinitive)
**It appears that Romy** has left early.

Nina seems **to be studying.** (present continuous infinitive)
**It seems that Nina** is studying.

He doesn't seem **to have been telling** the truth. (perfect continuous infinitive)
**It seems that** he was not telling the truth.

The verb **"help"** can be **followed by either bare or full infinitive**

I'm trying to **help you (to) understand** English grammar.

## purpose clauses **to express purpose**

**in order to+full infinitive and so as to+ full infinitive in formal English:**

We left early **in order to/ so as to** catch the bus.
(=We left early **to catch** the bus.)

We left early **in oder not to/so as not to** miss the bus.
(negative construction for both formal and informal Eglish)

**but**

**so that+full sentence, with a modal verb when there is a change of subject:**

We left early **so that we could catch** the bus.

**be the first/second/last/best,** etc +full infinitive

He was **the last** person **to enter** the room.

**"only" We use the infinitive after "only" to express annoyance**

He came home **only to find** that his house was robbed/broken into.

## some adjectives+infinitive

| be amazed | be disgusted | be sad |
|---|---|---|
| be angry | be eager | be unwilling |
| be apt | be happy | be willing |
| be bound | be obliged | it is important |
| be delighted | be prepared | it is necessary |
| be determined | be reluctant (unwilling) | it is vital |
| be difficult/hard | be prone | it is essential etc |

She's **prone to** exaggerate
(=She has the tendency to exaggerate.)

**I was surprised** to see him.
( =I was surprised when I saw him.)

He **was reluctant to help** me.
(=He didn't want to help me.)

Mary/she **is likely/ bound to help** us.

(=Mary will probably help us.)

**but**

**It is likely that Mary will help us.**

**be difficult (for me/you/him/her/us/them) to do something**

**It was difficult for me to understand** some teachers.

**find something difficult to do**

**I found it difficult to understand** some teachers.

but

**have difficulty (in) doing sth**

**I had difficulty in understanding** some teachers.

after adjectives **it's important, it's essential, it's vital, it's urgent, it's necessary,** we use **full infinitive when we have one subject**

It's important **to talk** to him.

**Note:** When we have another subject after it's important, it's urgent, it's vital etc we use a **that clause + the bare infinitive.**

It's important **that she talk** to him.

It is vital **that he follow** the doctor's advice.

### some nouns

| |
|---|
| have the ability |
| have the energy |
| have the money |
| have the means |
| have the need |
| have the potential |
| have the strength |
| have the time etc |
| have the urge (a strong wish) |

I have the money to buy a car.

I don't have the energy to exercise.

### too/enough+adjective

**too+ adjective+ (for me/him/her/ you etc.) to do sth**

It was **too cold** for **me to go** out.

**adjective+ enough + to do sth**

It **wasn't warm enough** for me **to go** out.

## (much) (far) too+adjective

### (much) (far) too+ adjective

It was **(much) (far) too cold**( for me) **to go** out.(=it was very cold, so I couldn't go out)

The chilly is( **much) too spicy to eat.**(=it was very spicy, so I couldn't eat it)

### but

### (much)(far) too much + uncountable noun

You put **(much) too much pepper** in the chilly. (=you put a lot of pepper in the chilly)

### (much)(far) too many + plural noun

There are **too many people** in this room,(=There are a lot of people in this room)

There are **much too many students** in this room.

You asked **far too many questions.**

### adjective + enough (for me/him/her/you/Ann etc )

The weather is not **warm enough to go** swimming.

Tim is not **old enough to go** out without an escort.

### it's time

It's time **to go** to sleep kids.

### verbs + an object pronoun or proper noun (me, you, him, her, it, us, you, them, Ann+full infinitive)

**I expect/want** you **to show** some understanding.

**I begged** her **not to tell.** ("not to do sth")(negative construction).

**He advised** me **to consult** a lawyer.

## Verb+object pronoun+full infinitive

| | | |
|---|---|---|
| **advise** | allow | appoint |
| **ask** | beg | bribe |
| **cause** | challenge | condemn |
| **convince** | dare | enable |
| **encourage** | expect | forbid |
| **force** | get | help |
| **implore** | incite | induce |
| **inspire** | instruct | invite |
| **mean** | order | pay |
| **permit** | persuade | recommend |
| **remind** | teach | tell |
| **urge** | want | warn |
| **wish** | would hate | would love |
| **would prefer** | | |

I **expect** you **to be** back on time for dinner.

Who **taught** you **to be** so cautious?

## be+too +adjective +(for me/him/her/you/Ann etc.)to do something

It was **too cold (for me) to go out.**

## adjective+ enough+ (for me/him/her/you/Ann etc.) to do something

It wasn't **warm enough (for me) to go out.**

## much (far)too+ adjective+ (for me/him/her/you/Ann/ etc.) to do something

It is **much too cold** (for me) to go out.(=it's very cold, so I can't go out)

The chilly is **much too spicy** (for me)to eat.(=it's very spicy ,so I can't eat it)

It's **far too late** (for us ) to catch a movie now.(=it's very late, so we should probably not go to the movies)

**Note:No infinitive is used after**:very-so-such-much-too much

It's very cold

**so+ adjective+ that+ full sentence:**

It was **so cold that I couldn't go out.**

**such+ a/an+adjective+singular countable noun(+ full sentence):**

It was **such a cold day** that I couldn't go out.

It was **such a lovely day** that we decided to go for a picnic.

**such +adjective+uncountable noun/plural noun(+ full sentence)**

It was **such a cold day** that I couldn't go out

*It was **such nice weather** that we decided to go on a picnic.

They are **such nice people** that you really should meet them.

*There's no article (a/an) before "weather" as "weather" is uncountable.
An article is not used before uncountable nouns and plural nouns.

**such+a lot of+uncountable noun/plural countable noun(+ full sentence)**

He won **such alot of money** on the lottery that he will probably not have to work for the rest of his life.

**so+ adjective +a+ noun+full sentence:**

It was **so cold a day** that I couldn't go out.

It was **so lovely a day** that we decided to go for a picnic.

**much (far) too much +uncountable noun (more than required):**

You put too much **pepper** in the chilly.(=you put a lot of pepper in the chilly)

You're carrying far too much **money** in your bag.

There's too much **sugar** in my coffee.

There's much too much **salt** in the soup.

**much(far) too many +plural noun (much more than necessary):**

There are much too many people in this room.(=there are a lot of people in this room)

## Expressing purpose

| | |
|---|---|
| **In order to do something** | **He studied hard** in order to do **well on the test.** |
| **So as to do something** | He studied hard **so as to do** well on the test. |
| **With a view to doing something** | He studied hard **with a view to doing** well on the test. |
| **With the aim of doing something** | He studied hard **with the aim of doing** well on the test. |
| **With the intention/hope of doing something** | He studied hard **with the intention of doing** well on the test. |
| **In the hope of doing something** | He studied hard **in the hope of doing** well on the test. |
| When we have a change of subject we use the construction: so that/ for fear that+ **subject+will, would,can,could,might** | He studied hard **so that he could/ would do** well on the test.<br>He studied hard **for fear that he might/would fail** the test. |

Helen Boubouli                              **Grammar Genie**

## It's time

| It's time **(for someone) to do** something | **It's time** to go **home.**<br>**It's time** ( for you) to do your homework**.** |
|---|---|
| It's time **someone did** something | **It's time** we went home.(unreal past)<br>**It's** time you did your homework.<br>**(the unreal simple past is used after it's time when there is a change of subject)** |

## It's about/high time

| ☑ **It's about/high time someone did** something<br><br>☒ ~~It's about/high time(for someone) to do something~~ | ☑**It's** (about/high) time you did your homework**. (unreal past)**<br><br>☒**It's (about/high) time to do** ~~your homework~~.(infinitives are not used with 'it's about/high time' ) |
|---|---|
| **Simple past(unreal past) is used after it's time, it's about time, it's high time.**<br>Past perfect is not possible because "it's time" refers to a present situation. ||

# BARE INFINITIVE

The bare infinitive is used with:

**modals (may, might, must, should, shall, would, will, can, could)**

You **should** work less.

**need, dare** (when used as auxiliary verbs)

You **needn't** get up early tomorrow.

We **daren't** tell her the truth.

expressions indicating **threats, warning, anger**

**Don't** you **dare raise** your voice to me again.

**How dare** you **hide** the truth from me.

**Always read** the instructions before you use an appliance for the first time.

**Never talk** to me like that again.

**Notes:** To express **courage** with **dare** we use **bare** or **full infinitive**

I **don't dare( to) go** outside in this weather.

**would rather/would sooner, had better**

**We'd better tell** her the truth.
(=We should tell her the truth)

**I would rather/would sooner watch** a comedy.(present & future reference) (=I prefer to watch a comedy)

**I would rather have watched a comedy.** (perfect infinitive for past reference)

Note: The unreal simple past or past perfect is used with would rather/would sooner when we have a change of subject:

I would rather/would sooner **you didn't lie** to me.

I would rather **you had come** earlier.

                **also:**

It would have been better if I had watched a comedy. ➲past (3rd conditional)

I would have preferred it if I had watched a comedy. ➲ past (3rd conditional)

## Would ratner=Would sooner

| When we have would rather/would sooner with 1 subject we use bare infinitive for the PRESENT+FUTURE ||
|---|---|
| I would rather do something<br>　　　bare infinitive | I would rather feed the dog.<br>　　　not feed the dog (negative) |
| **When we have would rather/would sooner with 1 subject we use perfect infinitive for the PAST** ||
| I would rather have done something<br>　　　perfect infinitive | I would rather have gone to the party.<br>　　　not have gone to the party (negative) |
| **When we have would rather/would sooner/would sooner with 2 subjects we use Simple Past(Unreal Past) for the PRESENT+FUTURE to show that we would like someone to do something for us.** ||
| I would rather you did something<br>Simple Past (unreal past) | I would rather you stopped talking.<br>I would rather you didn't make me feel bad.(negative)<br>I would rather you came with us tomorrow. |
| **When we have would rather/would sooner with 2 subjects we use Past Perfect(Unreal Past) for the PAST to show that we wish we had done or that we had not done something.** ||
| I would rather you had done something Past perfect (unreal past) | I would rather you had told me the truth.<br>I would rather you hadn't lied to me. (negative) |
| Also:It would have been better if+ past perfect: | It would have been better if you had done something. |

### it's important, it's necessary:

Is it necessary **to attend** this lecture?

It is important **to understand** what you have to do in case of emergency.

### verbs followed by an object + bare infinitive:

I **saw** the burglar **break into** the house.

### let :

The parents sometimes **let** their kids **stay up** late on week ends. ⊃active voice

### In passive voice the verb "allow" +full infinitive" is used instead of "let":

The kids are sometimes **allowed to stay up** late on week ends. ⊃passive voice

### help ⊃both a bare or full infinitive are used in active voice with no change in meaning, while in passive voice only a full infinitive is possible:

Pauline helped Mary **(to)tidy** her room. ⊃active voice

Mary was helped **to tidy** her room. ⊃passive voice

### make⊃a bare infinitive is used in active voice, while in passive voice we use a full infinitive:

The teacher made us **stay** after school. ⊃active voice

We were made **to stay** after school. ⊃passive voice

With **make, help, hear, feel** and **see** we use **bare infinitive** in **active voice** and **full infinitive** in **passive voice**:

| Active voice | Passive voice |
|---|---|
| Mrs. Jones **makes her children go** to bed early. | Mrs. Jones' children **are made to go** to bed early. |
| **We heard you lie** to your parents. | **You were heard to lie** to your parents. |
| **I helped you lift** the box. | **You were helped to lift** the box. |
| The neighbours **saw you come home** drunk. | **You were seen to come home** drunk. |

**Let becomes allow in passive voice:**

My boss **let** me **have** the day off. (active voice)

I was **allowed to have** the day off.(passive voice)

✗ I was let to have the day off

**Have someone do something in causative:**

I **had** my tutor **proof read** my short story.

Sheila **had** her sister **do** her homework.

Helen Boubouli                                  Grammar Genie

**Used to** + bare infinitive ➲ past habits/facts/states
**Would**+ bare infinitive➲ past habits/facts /not states

We use **"used to"** to talk about **actions and states** that happened repeatedly **in the past** that don't happen any more. We use **"would"** to talk about **actions** that happened **in the past, but not states.**

**I used to live in America.** ➲state(I don't live in America any more.**)**

✗ I would live in America. ➲wrong because the verb "live" is a stative verb

**I used to be an accountant.** ➲state (I'm not an accountant any more.)

✗ I would be an accountant. ➲**wrong because the verb to be is a stative verb**

When I was a student **I used to wake up** early to go to school. ➲action

When I was a student **I would wake up** early to go to school.➲action

(Both "I used to wake up early"… and "I would wake up early"…. mean that I don't wake up early any more.)

✓**I used to own a yacht**➲state
✗ I would own a yacht
✓**I used to like you**➲state
✗ I would like you

(We use **"would"** to talk about **actions** that happened in the past, but **not states)**.

You **cannot use "would" to ask questions.** You use **used to instead:**

✗ Would you wake up early when you were a student?

✓ Did you use to wake up early when you were a student?

**Would in the negative changes the meaning of the sentence:**

When I was younger **I would not smoke.**

(=I refused to smoke.)

        **but:**

When I was younger **I did not use to smoke.**

(=I didn't smoke then, but I do now.)

### be used to/be accustomed to

Be used to/be accustomed to+ ing ⮕ Present habits
Be used to/be accustomed to+noun

I'm used to waking up early in the morning.
I'm used to him.

### get used to/get accustomed to

Get used to /get accustomed to+ noun ⮕ Try to acquire the habit of doing something
Get used to/get accustomed to +ing

I'm trying to get used to leaving here.
I can't get used to our new teacher.
**(see page 25 for more on be used to/get used to)**


**It's important, vital, essential + full infinitive** with 1 subject:

**It's important to talk to him.**

When we have another subject after **"it's important, vital, essential"** etc we use subject pronoun + bare infinitive:

**It's important (that) he do something.**

## RELATIVE CLAUSES

### Defining relative clauses

**A defining relative clause gives important information about a person, thing or place and therefore cannot be separated by a comma from the main clause:**

This is the girl **who/that** won the contest.

The man **who/that** saved us happens to be our next door neighbour.

The woman **who/that** is standing by the door is our English teacher.

**Note**: the relative pronoun **"that"** can be used to replace **who, whom, or which in defining clauses.**

**In defining relative clauses when the relative pronoun is the object of the relative clause, it can be omitted:**

This is the guy (**who/that**) Michael was telling you about.

This is the house (**which/that**) they robbed.

Note: The relative pronoun is an object pronoun if it is followed by a noun, or subject pronoun instead of a verb:

This is the new car **(which/that)** I bought.**(object pronoun)**

Note: The relative pronoun is a subject pronoun if it is the subject of the verb:

Luggage **which/that** is unattended will be discarded.**(subject pronoun)**

**When the relative pronoun is the subject of the relative clause, it can not be omitted:**

This is the girl **who/that** excelled in high school.

This is the house **which/that** was robbed.

**The defining relative clause can be replaced by a participle:**

The view from the house **which is overlooking** the park is breathtaking. (=the view from the house **overlooking** the park is breathtaking.)(present participle)

The boy **who is running down** the street is my grandson. (=the boy **running down** the street is my grandson.)(present participle)

Most of the people **who were invited** to the party showed up late.(=Most of the people **invited** to the party showed up late.)(past participle)

## Relative pronouns used in defining relative clauses:

**Relative pronouns**

| | |
|---|---|
| **people** | who/that whom |
| **objects/animals** | which/that |
| **possessions** | whose |

**Relative adverbs**

| | |
|---|---|
| **place** | where |
| **time** | when |
| **reason** | why |

**Who/that** is used for people:

This is the guy **who** I was talking about.

**Which** is used for things and animals:

This is the house **(which)** I wanted to buy.

**Where** is used for places:

This is the place **where** I live.

The house **where** I was brought up is going to be demolished.

☒ The house **where** I was brought up ~~in/at~~ is going to be demolished.

The house **in/at which** I was brought up is going to be demolished.

The house **which** I was brought up **at/in** is going to be demolished.

The house **that** I was brought up **at/in** is going to be demolished.

The house I was brought up **in/at** is going to be demolished.

**That** can be used for people animals and things to replace who, **whom, which, where**, in defining relative clauses:

This is the guy ( **who/that)** I was talking about.

**When** is used for time:

Do you remember the day **(when)** we first went out?

**Whom** is used for people when it refers to the object of the verb, usually preceded by a preposition in formal English:

These are the people **about whom** I was telling you.

These are the people **(who/whom)** I was telling you **about.**

☒ This is the guy **whom** likes me. (whom should not be used when we are refering to the subject of the verb.)

☑ This is the guy **who** likes me.

☒ This is the girl **whom** excelled in high school.

☑ This is the girl **who/that** excelled in high school.

The use of **whom** not preceded by a preposition is unusual but possible:

This is my sister **who/whom** I trust.(=I trust my sister)

**The following constructions are used in formal English:**

This is the man **with whom** I collaborate.
This is the man **whom** I collaborate **with.**
This is the man **who** I collaborate **with.(less formal)**
This is the man **that** I collaborate **with.(informal)**
This is the man I collaborate **with.(informal)**

This is the girl **to whom** I was talking.
This is the girl **whom** I was talking **to.**
This is the girl **who** I was talking **to.(less formal)**
This is the girl **that** I was talking t**o.(informal)**
This is the girl I was talking to.**(informal)**

This is the house **in which** I lived.
This is the house **which** I lived **in.**
This is the house **that** I lived **in.(less formal)**
This is the house **where** I lived. **(informal)**
This is the house I lived in. **(informal)**

**Note:** Only **whom** and **which are used after a preposition:**

This is the girl **to whom** I was talking.

This is the house **in/at which** I lived.

The **relative pronoun can be omitted** only in defining relative clauses where it is the object of the relative clause:

This is the new car **(which/that)** I bought. **(object pronoun)**

This is the girl **(who/that)** I was talking to. **(object pronoun)**

Luggage **which/that** is unattended will be discarded.**(When the relative pronoun is a subject pronoun it cannot be omitted.)**

**Whose** is used both **for people and things** followed by a noun to show possession, **replacing his, her, its, their:**

This is the couple **whose** house was robbed.(=their house was robbed)

This is the couple **the house of whom** was robbed.

This is the house **whose** roof was blown away by the wind.(=its roof was blown away)

This is the house **the roof of which** was blown away by the wind.

**Why/that**

The reason **(why/that)** I'm late is because there was a terrible traffic jam.

Tell me the reason **(why/that)** you are not coming.

## Non-defining relative clauses

A non-defining clause gives extra information, about a person or thing, which is not necessary in understanding the meaning of a sentence. It can be separated from the main clause by a comma without causing any confusion:

My grandparents, **who** are retired, live in the countryside.

That house, **whose** roof was blown away by the wind, used to be beautiful.

I told him to be on time, **which** might be the reason why he showed up early.

**Note: the relative pronoun "that" is not used to replace who, whom or which in non-defining clauses.**

☑ Maria, **who** is my sister's best friend, has invited us to her birthday party.

☒ Maria, **that** is my sister's best friend, has invited us to her birthday party.

**The relative pronoun cannot be omitted in non-defining relative clauses even if it refers to the object of the relative clause:**

I advised him to try to seem more assertive, **which** I think was what contributed to his being hired.

*Note:* Relative pronouns used in non-defining relative clauses: **who, which, most of whom, which, whose**

Non-defining relative clauses can be introduced by the following expressions:

**Most of whom/which**
**Some of whom/which**
**All of whom/which**
**None of whom/which**
**Many of whom/which**
**One/two/three etc of whom/which**
**Half of whom/which**
**Each of whom/which**
**Neither of whom/which**
**Either of whom/which**

I have been to a lot of countries. Many of them are in Europe.(=I have been to a lot of countries, **many of which** are in Europe.)

A lot of people attended the meeting. Some of them I had never met before.(=A lot of people attended the meeting, **some of which** I had never seen before.)

I have met some interesting people in my trip to London. Half of them were from Greece.(=I have met some interesting people in my trip to London, **half of whom** were from Greece.)

A lot of people were injured in the accident. Most of them were children.(=A lot of people were injured in the accident, **most of whom** were children.)

There have been a lot of complaints about the food at that restaurant. One of them was from me. (=There have been a lot of complaints about the food at that restaurant, **one of which** was from me.)

## LINKING WORDS (CONJUNCTIONS)

Linking words (conjunctions) are used to join words together. There are more conjunctions in English than in any other language, so the ability to use them correctly is very important.

**A dependant clause or a subordinate clause** is a clause that depends on the main clause for its meaning. When the sentence begins with a subordinating conjunction we have a dependant or a subordinate clause.

When we have a dependent(subordinate) clause first in a sentence followed by an independent clause we use a comma to separate them:

**In spite of** having fallen behind, I managed to catch up.

I managed to catch up in spite of having fallen behind.(no comma)

**Clause**= A clause contains a subject and a verb.

He was sleeping, so I left

**Dependent or subordinate clause**=It is a clause that depends on another for it's meaning.

Because he was sleeping**, I left.**

**Independent clause**=It can stand on it's own and does not depend on another for its meaning. For this reason it is often called a sentence and not necessarily a clause. It is correct to use a comma to join two independent clauses together.

He was watching television , so I decided to work on my essay.

**Subordinating conjunction**=it is a word that joins a dependent clause to an independent clause.
It comes at the beginning of a dependent clause or at the end of an independent one, between the dependent and the independent clause.

In spite of having fallen behind, I managed to catch up.

I managed to catch up in spite of having fallen behind.

**Co-ordinating conjunction (short conjunction)**= a) is used to join independent clauses together and is usually preceded by a comma b) does not require a comma if the independent clauses are short.

Sunny was sleeping, so I left.

I saw Bill and I ran up to him.

**Correlative conjunctions**= Correlative conjunctions are pairs of words that are used to connect two things which have a strong influence on each other.

I can't decide whether to tell her or not.

I like both her appearance and her personality.

## Subordinating Conjunctions
## Clauses of result

Result clauses, introduced by conjunctions of result, are used to show the result of an action or a situation.

**so+ adjective/adverb +that+ full sentence**

It was so cold that I couldn't go out.

**such+ a/an+adjective+singular countable noun(+ full sentence)**

It was **such a cold day** that I couldn't go out.

It was **such a lovely day** that we decided to go for a picnic.

**such +adjective+uncountable noun/plural noun(+ full sentence)**

*It was **such nice weather** that we decided to go on a picnic.

They are **such nice people** that you really should meet them.

*There's no article before "weather" as "weather" is uncountable.
An article is not used before uncountable nouns and plural nouns.

**such+a lot of+uncountable noun/plural countable noun(+ full sentence)**

I have such a lot of money that I don't need to work.

Such a lot of people attended the concert that the stadium was packed.

**so +adjective +a/an+count singular noun**

*It was **so cold a day** that I couldn't go out.

*The above construction is used with countable singular nouns only.

**so few/ many+plural countable noun+(that)+ full sentence**

I have **so many friends that** I always have someone to turn to.

**so little/ much/+uncountable noun+(that)+ full sentence**

I have **so little time** that I have to ask you to leave.

He has **so much money** that he's giving away some to charity.

**as a result**

No one showed up for the lecture; **as a result** it was cancelled.

No one showed up for the lecture. **As a result** it was cancelled.

**(and) as a result**

No one showed up for the lecture**, and as a result** it had to be cancelled.

No one showed up for the lecture and it had to be cancelled **as a result**.

**as a result of +noun or ing** (because of)

**As a result of** poor attendance the lecture had to be cancelled.

**with the result that+ clause**

No one showed up for the lecture, **with the result that** it had to be cancelled.

**resulting in+ing or noun**

No one showed up for the lesson, **resulting in** its cancellation/being cancelled.

**and consequently +clause**

No one showed up for the lecture, and **consequently/in consequence** it had to be cancelled.

**as a consequence + clause**

No one showed up for the lecture, and **as a consequence/as a result** it had to be cancelled.

No one showed up for the lecture and it had to be cancelled **as a consequence**.

**(and)in consequence+clause**

No one showed up for the lecture **and in consequence** had to be cancelled.

No one showed up for the lecture. **In consequence** it had to be cancelled.

**for this/that reason**

No one showed up for the lecture. **For this reason** it had to be cancelled.

**(and) therefore(used to introduce the result of something)**

No one showed up for the lecture , **and therefore** had to be cancelled.

No one showed up for the lecture. **Therefore,** it had to be cancelled.

**thus (=as a result of something mentioned)(formal)**

No one showed up for the lecture , **and thus** had to be cancelled.

**so**

No one showed up for the lecture, **so** it was cancelled.

**hence +noun(=for this reason/ that is the reason for/therefore)** very formal

He's taking an oath today, **hence** the formal attire.(=he's dressed formally because he's taking an oath today)

Being hard working helps you develop your personality, **and hence** your image.(=you develop your image as a result of working hard)

No one showed up for the lecture, **and hence** the cancellation.

No one showed up for the lecture, **hence** the cancellation. (=the cancellation is a consequence of poor attendance)

## Purpose Clauses

| | |
|---|---|
| to do **something** | not to do something |
| **in order(for someone)** to do something | **in order not to do** something |
| **so as** to do something | **so as not to do** something (formal) |
| **with a view** to doing **something** | to avoid **doing** something |
| with the intention/hope of doing something | **for fear** of doing something |
| in the hope of doing something | **When we have a change of subject we can use the construction:**<br><br>**lest he (should )do** sth➲**subjunctive**<br><br>**Being rather formal, however, its use is rather rare.**<br>**The following construction is more frequent:** |
| with the aim of doing something | **for fear that he will,would,can,could, may,might do sth**<br>**(for fear that+subject+will, would, can, could, may,might +bare infinitive)** |

The following are used both in affirmative and negative constructions when there is a change of subject:
so that+subj+will,would,can,could,may,might
in the hope that+subject+will, would,can, could, may , might

**Affirmative informal constructions:**

He studied hard **to do** well on the test.

**Affirmative formal constructions:**

He studied hard **in order to do** well on the test.

He studied hard **so as to do** well on the test.

He studied hard **with a view to doing** well on the test.

He studied hard **with the intention of doing** well on the test.

He studied hard **in the hope of doing** well on the test.

He studied hard **with the aim of doing** well on the test.

**Negative formal constructions:**

He studied hard **in order not to fail** the test.

He studied hard **to avoid failing** the test.

He studied hard **for fear of failing** the test.

He studied hard **for fear that he would not do well** on the exam.

He studied hard **lest he (should) fail** the test. (subjunctive)

**"lest", "So that", "in the hope that" and "for fear that" require a change of subject:**

**He** studied hard **so that his parents** would be pleased.

**He** studied hard **in the hope that his parents** would be pleased. **(=He** studied hard **so as/ in order to please his parents**.)
**(=He** studied hard **in the hope of pleasing his parents**.)

Alex stayed after **so that his teacher could** explain something that he didn't understand.

Alex stayed after **in the hope that his teacher could** explain something that he didn't understand. (=Alex stayed after **in order for the teacher to explain** something that he didn't understand.)

**The same subject is also possible:**

**He** studied hard **so that he** could do well on the test.**(=He** studied hard **so as /in order to do** well on the test.)

**He** studied hard **lest he (should) fail** the test.(subjunctive)

**He** studied hard **for fear that he would fail** the exam. .**(=He** studied hard **in order not /so as not to fail** on the test.)

**Also:**
**for+ing=to describe the purpose of sth and what it's used for:**

This pan is (used) **for frying fish.**

86

**for+noun=to describe why someone does something:**

He's doing this job **for the money**.

**in case(subordinating conjunction) +simple present for the present and the future.**

Take an umbrella **in case it rains**.

Take an umbrella **in case it should rain**.

**Note:** ➲ "will" or "would" are not used after "In case"
**in case+present perfect**

Remind him **in case he has forgotten**.

**in case+simple past for the past:**

I took an umbrella **in case it rained**.

**"not to" is not used for a negative purpose:**

❌ He studied hard not **to fail** the test. ➲ "not to" is not used for a negative purpose

☑ He studied hard **so as not to fail** the test.

❌ He left early not to miss the bus.

☑ He left early **in order  not to** miss the bus.

## Time and Condition Clauses

Time clauses introduced by time and condition conjunctions, are used to indicate **when or why something happens.**

A comma is used when the time clause or the condition clause comes before the main clause.

It is used when we have a subordinate (dependent) clause followed by an independent clause.

A comma is not used when the time clause or the condition clause comes after the main clause. (It is not used when we have an independent clause followed by a dependent clause).

❌We'll serve dinner, as soon as you come home.

✅**As soon as you** come **home,** we'll serve dinner.

**Future tenses "Will" or "Would" "going to +infinitive" are not used after time and condition conjunctions. Future tenses are however used in the main clause.**

❌As soon as you ~~will come~~ home, **we'll** serve dinner.

❌As soon as you ~~are going to come~~ home, **we'll** serve dinner.

✅As soon as you **come** home, **we'll** serve dinner.

"When" used as a question word **does take future tenses:**

**When** will you see him? (question word)

**When** are we going to have the party? (question word)

"When" used as a time conjunction **does not take future tenses:**

❌ **When** you ~~will come~~ home, we'll serve dinner.(time conjunction)

☑ **When** you **come** home, we'll serve dinner.(time conjunction)

"If" after **I wonder, I doubt, I don't know, I'm not sure**, etc.can also be followed by future tenses:

**I don't know if I will apply** for this job after all.

**I wonder if she will tell** her parents that she failed the test again.

After time conjunctions **we use present tenses to refer to the future.** We may use future or imperative in the main clause:

I'll come with you **provided (that)** we are back before midnight.

**Supposing** we buy a house in the country- will that please you?

Take an umbrella **in case** it rains.

After time conjunctions we use **past tenses to refer to the past:**

I took an umbrella **in case** it rained.

**Immediately** she had left the building, there was an explosion.(British English)
(**As soon** as she left the building,...)

**Ever since** Anna came back from the island, she has been miserable.

We are not required to use past perfect after "after" and "before" for the action that happened first since the order of events is clearly indicated by the conjunctions:

The postman came **after** I(had )left.

She went to bed **before** I had come home.

or

She went to bed **before** I came home.

We do, however, use past perfect in the main clause to indicate that something happened before something else:

**When** I came home, **she had gone** to bed.

| **TIME CLAUSES** | **CONDITION CLAUSES** |
|---|---|
| after | on condition that |
| as long as | as long as |
| as soon as | provided/providing that |
| immediately(British):as soon as | only if |
| before | suppose/supposing that |
| until | even if/though |
| by the time | if |
| | unless |
| | in case |
| the minute/ the moment | |
| (the)next time | |
| the sooner..the.. | |
| once | |
| until/till | |
| (ever) since | |
| when | |
| whenever | |
| while | |
| whilst (formal) | |

**"While"** and **"as"** followed by continuous tenses to emphasize the **duration of an action:**

She sneaked in the auditorium **while** the professeur **was giving** a lecture.

**While I was taking** a shower, I heard you come in.

You interrupted me **while I was talking.**

**"While"** can also be used to describe **two actions happening at the same time:**

**While I'm talking** to you, **you're reading** the newspaper.

**Peter is watching** television **while Ann is studying** for her test.

**While the professeur was giving** a lecture, **the students were taking** notes.

**You were knocking** on the door **while I was taking** a shower.

**"When" can also be used to describe two actions happening at the same time:**

**When I'm talking** to you, **you're reading** the newspaper.

**When I was working, you were sleeping.**

**You were sleeping when I was working.**

**"When" + simple past is used to describe a shorter action that interrupted a longer one:**

I was taking a shower **when the telephone rang.**

**By/Until
"By" =(not after) Something has to be done before a certain point. "By" gives a dead line:**

You have to hand in your composition **by** Friday.(You can't hand in your composition after Friday.)

**"Until"= (not after) "Until" emphasises how long something continuous before it is completed at a certain point:**

You have **until** Friday to hand in your composition.(=You can't hand in your composition after Friday.)

Don't buy me that shirt I told you I liked **until** I give you the money.(=Don't buy it before I give you the money.)

## Clauses of Concession or Contrast Clauses

A contrast clause, introduced by a conjunction of contrast, is used in order to indicate something which contrasts with something else, the result of which is unexpected.

If the conjunctions under this category come before the main clause, we use a comma to separate the two clauses. When we have a dependent clause subordinate first in a sentence followed by an independent clause we use a comma to separate them:

**although/even though/though +clause(subject+verb)**

**Although/Even though** I'm wealthy, I refuse to waste my money.

I refuse to waste my money **even though** I'm wealthy.

**We can also put "though" at the end of the sentence:**

I'm wealthy. I refuse to waste my money **though.**

**Despite/In spite of +noun or gerund**

**In spite of the fact that +clause(subject+verb)**

**Despite the fact that+clause(subject+verb)**

**Despite** being wealthy, I refuse to waste my money.

I refuse to waste my money **despite** being wealthy.

I refuse to waste my money **despite the fact that** I'm wealthy.

| Adjective / adverb + though/as + clause(used for emphasis) |

**Rich though/as** I am/might be, I refuse to waste my money.(=Even though I'm rich, I refuse to waste my money.)

**Much as** I would like to come with you, I'm afraid I can't.(Even though I would like to come with you, I'm afraid I can't)

**Beautifully though/as** she sings, she is not well known.(=Although she sings beautifully, she is not well known.)

| Bare infinitive + as + subject + may / might |

**Try as I might**, I didn't make it in time for dinner.(=Even though I tried, I didn't make it in time for dinner.)

**Try as you may**, you will not be able to convince him.(=In spite of how hard you try, you will not be able to convince him.)

nevertheless
nonetheless
however...(still)
albeit

The party was fun, **albeit** a little quiet.

He came, **albeit** without the notes that I had asked him to bring.

**We always use a comma after: however, nonetheless, nevertheless**

I'm quite rich; **nevertheless,** I refuse to waste my money.

I'm quite rich; **nonetheless,** I refuse to waste my money.

I'm quite rich; **however**, I refuse to waste my money.

If the conjunction is in the middle of the sentence, we use two commas:

I'm quite rich. I refuse, **however,** to waste my money.

**even so**
**all the same**
**but...still**

**yet...(still)**
**still**
**(and)yet**

I'm quite rich; **even so,** I refuse to waste my money.

I'm quite rich; **all the same,** I refuse to waste my money.

I'm quite rich**, but** I refuse to waste my money.

I'm quite rich, **but I still** refuse to waste my money.

Although I'm quite rich, I **still** refuse to waste my money.

I'm quite rich. **Still,** I refuse to waste my money.

I'm quite rich, **(and) yet I** refuse to waste my money.

I'm quite rich, **but** I refuse to waste my money **anyway**.

He studies little, **yet** he does well in school.

He writes very fast, **yet** legibly.

He's quite rich, **yet** unwilling to spend money.

**no matter how** +adjective/adverb+clause

**however** +adjective/adverb+clause

**no matter what** +clause

**whatever+clause**

**No matter how** rich I am/might be, I refuse to spend my money on useless things.

**However** rich I am/might be, I refuse to spend my money on useless things.

**No matter what** he says/might say, I don't believe him.

**Whatever** he says/might say, I don't believe him.

**but**
**while+clause**
**where(as)**
**whilst (used in formal or literary English)**

**While** I might be rich, I refuse to spend my money on useless things.

I am self confident, **where(as) /while** he is very shy.

I am rich, **but** I refuse to spend my money on useless things.

**on the one hand**(used at the beginning of the first sentence)
**on the other hand**(used at the beginning of the second sentence)
**in contrast to**+noun
**contrary to**+noun
**on the contrary** (used between two sentences)

   **(Even) though/Although** it was raining, we went out.

It was raining. We went out **though.**

**Despite** the rain, we went out.

**In spite of** the rain, we went out

We went out **in spite of** the rain.

We went out **in spite of the fact that** it was raining.

It was raining. **Nevertheless,** we went out.

It was raining**; nonetheless,** we went out.

It was raining. **However**, we went out.

It was raining. **However,** we (**still**) went out

It was raining**, but** we went out.

It was raining**, but we still** went out.

It was raining**, but** we went out **anyway.**

It was raining**, yet** we **still** went out.

It was raining. **Still** we went out.

I'm learning English, **but** Helen is learning Chinese

I'm learning Chinese, **where as** Helen is not.

I'm learning English, **while** Helen is learning Chinese.

I'm learning English, **where (as)** Helen is learning Chinese.

**Where (as**) Helen is learning Chinese, I'm learning English.

**While** Helen is learning Chinese, I'm learning English

I'm learning English**; however**, Helen is learning Chinese.

I'm learning English; Helen is learning Chinese, **however.**

I'm learning English; Helen, **on the other hand**, is learning Chinese.

## Reason Clauses

Reason clauses, introduced by conjunctions of reason, can be used in order to explain **why something happens.**

| | |
|---|---|
| because | |
| for=because (old-fashioned or literary) | |
| since | |
| as | +clause |
| the reason why | |
| seeing that | |
| on the grounds that | |
| due to the fact that | |
| in view of the fact that | |

We listened eagerly **because** he brought good news.

We listened eagerly **for** he brought good news.

**Because** John wanted to get into a good university, he studied really hard.

John was studying really hard **because** he wanted to get into a good university.

**Since** John wanted to get into a good university, he studied really hard.

John studied really hard **since** he wanted to get into the university.

**As** john wanted to get into a good university, he studied really hard.

**The reason for** studying hard was that John wanted to get into a good university.

**The reason (why)** John studied hard was that he wanted to get into a good university.

**Seeing that** it was difficult to get into a good university, John studied really hard.

The case was dismissed **in view of the fact that** there was not enough evidence.

**Due to the fact that /In view of the fact that** john wanted to get into a good university, he studied really hard.

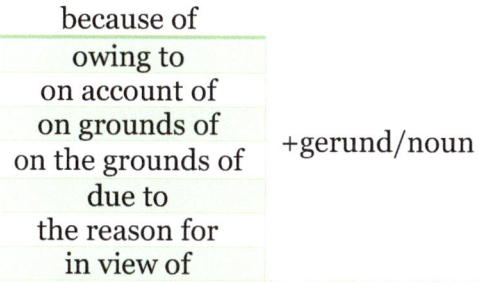

**Because of** the problems at home, I couldn't do any homework.

I couldn't do any homework **because of** the problems at home.

**Owing to/due to/on account of** adverse weather conditions, all flights were cancelled.

The lecture was cancelled **on the grounds that** there was no attendance.

The lecture was cancelled **on grounds of** poor attendance.

His prison sentence had been reduced **due to** extenuating circumstances.

His prison sentence had been reduced **on grounds of** extenuating circumstances.

**hence+noun(for this reason/ that is the reason for/therefore)** very formal

He's taking an oath today, **hence** the formal attire.(He's taking an oath today. That's why he's dressed formally.)

Being hard working helps you develop your personality **and hence** your image.

### Adding information

| in addition to | |
| apart from (formal) | |
| except(for) | + gerund/noun |
| besides(informal) | |
| as well( as) | |
| let alone | |

**In addition to owning** a lot of property, he has a lot of money in the bank.

**Apart from owning** a lot of property, he has a lot of money in the bank.

**Except for Mary**, who was suspended, everybody else is here.

Invite Helen, and john **as well.**

I want to visit Italy **as well as** France.

Don't you have any other interests **besides /apart from** working out?

**Besides/apart from** working out, don't you have any other interests?

|  |  |
|---|---|
| on top of that (informal) | |
| in any case (informal) | **+ clause** |
| not to mention (formal) | |

I spent one hour waiting for the bus, **not to mention** that I was soaking wet by the time I got home.

I had to work overtime today, **on top of that** I missed the bus and had to wait one hour for the next one.

### anyway (informal)

Maria didn't want to go to school today, but she went **anyway.**

We didn't want to go, but we went **anyway.**

I don't think I'm going to buy this outfit. I can't afford it, **anyway.**

**The following expressions are used in formal English to add information. They are separated from the rest of the sentence with a comma.**

| |
|---|
| furthermore |
| moreover |
| what's more |
| in addition |

You're going to be late for your interview. **Moreover**, your casual attire is wholly inappropriate.

| |
|---|
| too/as well/ also/ still |
| not only...but also |
| not only...but...as well |
| neither...nor |
| either...or |
| both...and |

I'm learning **both** English **and** Chinese.

I want to buy **either** the brown bag **or** the black one.

I like **neither** the black **nor** the brown one.

**Not only** is Helen learning English **but** ( she's learning) Chinese too/as well.

Helen is **not only** learning Chinese **but** ( she's learning) English too/as well.

Helen is learning **not only** Chinese **but** ( she's learning) English too/as well.

**Not only** is Helen learning English **but** she's **also** learning Chinese.

## Clauses of manner

as
as if/as though
in a way
in the way                              +clause
just as
like
much as
the way

---

The house looks **as if** it has been broken into.(it probably has)

You act **as if/though** I didn't inform you.

You act **as if** you were the boss.

You looked **as if** you had won the lottery.( Past perfect is used when the imaginary action of the "**as if**" clause happened before the action of the main clause.)

**Much as** I like you, I can't give out confidential information.(Even though I like you, I can't give out confidential information).

> After **as if/as though** we use **simple past or past continuous for an unlikely situation in the present**
> If we want to talk about a situation that is probable in the present we usually use a present or future tense.
> It is commonly used **after the verbs look, sound, seem, appear, be, treat, behave, feel, act.**

**As if/as though + present, future tense⇒probable situation in the present**

You act **as if/as though you are** the boss. (is it possible that you are?)

You are acting **as if/as though you are** American (is it possible that you are?)

You treat me **as if/as though I have done** something to you.(have I done something?)

It looks **as if/as though it's going to rain**.(it might rain)

It doesn't seem **as if/as though she's going to come**.(she will probably not come)

You look **as if you're lying.** (you're probably lying.)

**As if/as though + simple past, past continuous⇒unlikely situation in the present**

You act **as if/as though you were** the boss.(it is unlikely that you are the boss)

You're acting **as if/as though you were** American (it is unlikely that you are American)

I remember what happened **as if/as though it were** yesterday.

You look **as if you were lying**.(you give the impression that you are lying even though you are not.)

**As if/as though + past perfect⇒unlikely situation in the past**

You act **as if/as though he had been** the one to treat you badly.(it is unlikely that he was the one)

In informal English **"like"** is usually used **instead of as if/ as though:**

You act **like** you were lying.(=it is unlikely that you are lying)

You act **like** you are the boss.=(is it possible that you are?)

It looks **like** she's going to be late.(=it is possible that he might be late)

He looks **like** he has been working all night.(=it is possible that he was working all night)

He looks **like** he had been working all night.=(this is the impression that he gives even though it is unlikely that he had been working all night)

## Conjunctions giving examples

**for instance**
**for example**
**in particular(especially)**

What would you do, **for instance,** if there was an earthquake?

In a recession, **for instance,** people are made redundant.

Can you tell me a little bit about yourself? **For instance** what do you do?

A lot of people, teenagers **for example,** like watching American soap operas.

It's not easy to be learning three languages at the same time, **for example** English, French and Chinese.

Is there anything **in particular** that you would like us to do tonight?

What **in particular** do you intend to do about your alcohol addiction?

Where do you want us to go for the weekend? No where in **particular**.

I'm not addressing anyone **in particular.**

## Conjunctions making exceptions

**except (for)/ apart from/besides +noun/ ing**

Everyone attended the meeting **except for/apart from/besides** Tonia.

**except(that)\except in/to/by**

No one should use this room **except in** some cases.

**except when/where/if**

I won't come **except if** you promise not to bring Tom along.

**except (to) do sth**

I don't want to do anything today, **except (to) lie** down in bed all day and rest.

**except (that)**

I came home after all, **except (that)** I was a little late.

**unlike +noun**

Helen is ambitious, **unlike** her sister.(her sister is not)

**Unlike** Maria, Paulina likes to stay home on weekends.

### rather than/instead(of)

Pauline decided to go ahead with the wedding **rather than** wait another year.

### unless=if not

We can't leave **unless** Veronica agrees to come with us.

### other than+ bare infinitive/noun

There's nothing to do tonight, **other than** stay home and watch television maybe.

Some people have nothing to say, **other than** rubbish.

## Coordinating Conjunctions(short conjunctions)

It is important to remember that a coordinating conjunction is a word that is used **to join two independent clauses** which are of equal importance, **and is usually preceded by a comma:**

I'm studying Spanish, **but** Dimitra is studying Italian.

I'm working on this grammar book, **so** I don't have much free time for anything else.

### Do not require a comma if the independent clauses are short:

I speak English and I'm learning Chinese.

### A comma is not used if the second clause doesn't state its subject:

He has finished writing the book but is still writing the article.

He has finished writing the book, but **he** is still writing the article.

> **A comma is optional if "and" is used before the last word of a list of nouns:**

Helen speaks English, Chinese, and French.
or
Helen speaks English, Chinese and French.

### Correlative Conjunctions (emhasizing two things)

**Correlative conjunctions are pairs of words that are used to connect two things which have a strong influence on each other.** An important point to remember when using correlative conjunctions is that **nouns must be used with other nouns, verbs with other verbs, adjectives with other adjectives, adverbs with other adverbs and so on.** The following are some of the commonest correlative conjunctions:

| | |
|---|---|
| **both...and** | I'm learning **both** English **and Chinese.** |
| **either...and** | I want to buy **either** the brown bag **or** the black one. |
| **neither...nor** | I like **neither** the black **nor** the brown one. |
| **not only...but...too/as well** | **Not only** is Helen learning English **but** (she's learning) Chinese too/as well. Helen is **not only** learning Chinese **but** (she's learning) English too/as well. Helen is learning **not only** Chinese **but** (she's learning) English too/as well. |
| **Not only...but also** | **Not only** is Helen learning English **but** she's **also** learning Chinese. |
| **whether...or** | I can't decide **whether** to go **or** stay. |
| **so...as** | You're not **as** smart **as** you think you are. |
| **just as...so** | You're **just as** unreliable **as** everybody else in this company. |
| **not...but** | You're **not** who you say you are **but** who you prove to be. |

**Famous quotations:**

"Those who would give up essential liberty to purchase a little temporary safety deserve **neither** liberty **nor** safety."
(Benjamin Franklin)

"To accomplish great things, we must **not only** act, **but also** dream; **not only** plan, **but also** believe."
(Anatole France)

"The man of knowledge must be able **not only** to love his enemies **but also** to hate his friends."
(Friedrich Nietzsche, Ecce Homo)

"Education is **not** the filling of a pail **but** the lighting of a fire."
(William Butler Yeats)

The fascination of shooting as a sport depends almost wholly on **whether** you are at the right **or** wrong end of the gun."
(P. G. Wodehouse)

"**Neither** the life of an individual **nor** the history of a society can be understood without understanding both."
(C. Wright Mills)

"In the end, we will remember **not** the words of our enemies **but** the silence of our friends."(Martin Luther King, Jr.)

"It is difficult to produce a television documentary that is **both** incisive **and** probing when every twelve minutes it is interrupted by twelve dancing rabbits singing about toilet paper."
(Rod Serling)

"**Either** you decide to stay in the shallow end of the pool **or** you go out in the ocean."(Christopher Reeve)

## CONDITIONALS
### Type 0
For general truths or situations or conditions which are always true

**If+ simple present, ➲ simple present**

If water freezes, it turns into ice.

If I don't eat anything one day, I get dizzy.

If I don't get enough sleep, I can't function.

When I study, I do well in tests.

### Type 1

**True or probable in the Present or Future**

| If+ Simple Present, present perfect, or present continuous | ➲ | will (future)/ simple Present/ can/ may/might/would+ bare infinitive/command (imperative) |
|---|---|---|

**If** I see you, I will tell you what happened.

I will tell you what happened If I see you. (without a comma)

**If** I wake up early, I have time to do a lot of things.

I have time to do a lot of things if I wake up early.

**If** I don't see Nina, I won't tell her the news.

If you finish early, you may/ go out and play.

## when / if:

**If I finish my work, I'll go shopping.**
(=If I don't finish my work, I won't go shopping.)

**When I finish my work, I'll go shopping.**
(=I will finish my work first, and then I'll go shopping.)

**If you come, we'll serve dinner.**
(=We will only serve dinner if you come. If you don't come, we won't.)

**When you come, we'll serve dinner.**
(=We won't serve dinner until you come. We'll wait for you to come, and then we'll serve dinner.)

> A comma is used when **the time clause or the condition clause comes before the main clause.**

**If** you see Dimitri, give him a kiss from me.

Give Dimitri a kiss from me if you see him.

> **"Will" is not used in conditionals with future meaning.**

Incorrect: If I will see Romy, I'll introduce her to you.

Correct: If I see Romy, I'll introduce her to you.

> **Will is used in polite conditionals**, but with caution.

Correct: I will really appreciate it if you **will** be kind enough to accompany me.

> **In polite requests we can use the future (will, should, might) or the present Conditional (would) in both clauses.**

I **will** attend the ceremony **if you will invite** all my associates. ⮕ less formal

I **would** be honored **if you would join me** for dinner. ⮕ formal

I **would/should** be grateful **if you would assist me** in this project.

**If you get off** work early, you **might** want to join us.

You **might** want to join us **if you get off** work early.

**"Unless" has a negative meaning**. That's why the verb that follows is always affirmative:

**Unless they invite me,** I won't go.
(=**If they don't invite me,** I won't go.)

I won't say anything **unless you tell me to.**
(=I won't say anything **if you don't tell me to.**)

With **"should"** the speaker is not sure.
The action is less probable. It is less likely to happen:

**If you should go** to the pharmacy, can you buy me some aspirins? (=The speaker will probably not go to the pharmacy.)

**This is similar to:**

**If you go/happen to go** to the pharmacy today, can you buy me some aspirins?

You can also **begin the sentence with "should"** followed by the subject instead of "if". This is called an inversion:

**Should you go** to the pharmacy, can you buy some aspirins for me?(=If you (should) go to the pharmacy, ......)

**Should you go** out in the rain, you will definitely catch a cold.(=If you (should) go out in the rain, .....)

## Type 2
**Unlikely, imaginary in the Present or Future**

| If+ Simple Past | ⮕ | would<br>could + bare infinitive<br>might |
|---|---|---|

**If I saw** Nina**, I would tell** her about the test.(=It is unlikely that I will see Nina)

**I would tell** Nina about the test **if I saw** her.

**If I won** a lot of money**, I would travel** around the world.(=I will probably not win a lot of money)

**I would travel** around the world **if I won** a lot of money.

> We use a comma only when we begin the sentence with "if"

### We don't use "would" after "if":

**Incorrect:** If I would see Nina, I would tell her about the test.

**Correct:** If I saw Nina, I would tell her about the test.

We can use **"were" in all persons**, singular & plural **with** the verb **"to be"** to express **improbability** like we use "should"in the first conditional:

**If he were/was rich**, he would donate a lot of money to charity.

**If I were/was you**, I would pay attention in class.

**With "were" we can only use action verbs and not state verbs:**

☒ If he were to believe you, would you be satisfied?(believe is a state verb)

☑ If he believed you, would you be satisfied?

☑If he were to apologise, would you forgive him? (apologise is an action verb)

**You can also begin the sentence with "were" instead of "if" followed by the subject. This is called an inversion:**

**Were I you,** I would be grateful. (=If I were you, ........)

**Were I you,** I would not give up so easily.(=If I were you, ..........)

**BUT FOR= If it wasn't for:**

**But for her mum,** she wouldn't know how to cook.(=**If it wasn't for** her mum, she wouldn't know how to cook.)

## Type 3
## Impossible, improbable about the Past

| If + Past Perfect | ➲ | would + have + past participle<br>could + have + past participle<br>might + have + past participle |
|---|---|---|

**If I had seen** Romy, **I would have invited** her to dinner.( =but I didn't see her so I didn't invite her)

**I would have gone** on the excursion **if I hadn't been** so ill. ( =but I was ill so didn't go)

**If we hadn't been** so lazy, **we could have done** so many things when we were young. (= we had the opportunity to do so many things then, but we were too lazy)

### We can also invert "past perfect" instead of using "if":

**Had I studied**, I would have passed the exam.(= If I had studied, I........)

### BUT FOR=If it hadn't been for:

**But for her husband's support**, she would never have succeeded. (=**If it hadn't been for** her husband's support, she would never have succeeded.)

**But for your advice**, I would probably have made the wrong choices in life. **(=If it hadn't been for your advice, I would probably have made the wrong choices in life. )**

# Progressive Verb Tenses in Conditionals

When the meaning we want to convey has continuity, we use continuous tenses.

## Type 1

If + Present Continuous
    or
Present perfect continuous

➲  will(future)/
will be+ing/
simple present/
can/may/might/would+bare infinitive/
imperative

**If it's not snowing**, I **will go** out.(=It might be snowing, so I will not go out.)

**If he's not watching T.V.**, he **will probably be** studying.(=He is either studying or watching television.)

**If you have been studying all night,** you **will be** tired today.(=I have a feeling that you have been studying all night.)

**If you have been lying** to me, **admit it** now.

## Type 2

**If + Past Continuous**

**True:** It is snowing, so I won't go outside.
**Conditional: If it were not snowing**, I would go outside.(= it's snowing so I won't go outside)

## Type 3

**If + Past Perfect Continuous**

**If she had been studying,** she would have passed the test. (=she wasn't studying, so she didn't pass the test)

### Mixed Conditionals

Various mixed combinations are possible if the meaning allows it.

| 3ʳᴰ CONDITIONAL | | 1ˢᵀ CONDITIONAL |
|---|---|---|
| If +past perfect continuous | ⤴ | will+bare infinitive<br>will be +ing |
| **3ʳᴰ CONDITIONAL** | | **2ᴺᴰ CONDITIONAL** |
| If+Past Perfect<br>or<br>If+Past Perfect Continuous | ⤴ | would/could/might + bare infinitive<br>or<br>would be+ ing |

         3ⁿᵈ                        2ⁿᵈ
**If he hadn't saved me from drowning, I wouldn't be alive.**
(=I'm alive because he saved me from drowning.)

         3ʳᵈ                        2ⁿᵈ
**If he hadn't been studying all night, he wouldn't be tired now.** (=He was studying all night. That's why he's tired now.)

         3ʳᵈ                        2ⁿᵈ
**If he hadn't gone out last night, he wouldn't be studying hard today.** (=He is studying hard today because he went out last night.)

         3ʳᵈ                        2ⁿᵈ
**If it had snowed, I would be shouting with joy now.**
(=I'm not shouting with joy, because it didn't snow.)

         3ʳᵈ                        2nd
**But for my teacher's support all these years, I wouldn't be who I am today.** (=**If it hadn't been for** my teacher's support all these years, I wouldn't be who I am today.)
(=I am who I am today because of my teacher's support.)

2ᴺᴰ CONDITIONAL          3ᴿᴰ CONDITIONAL
**If+Simple Past/past continuous ⊃ would have+past participle**

       2ⁿᵈ                                       3ʳᵈ
**If you were not sick, I would not have come to see you.**
  (=I came to see you because you are sick.)

      2ⁿᵈ                                  3ʳᵈ
**If I didn't have a lot of work, I wouldn't have come to work early.**(=I came to work early because I have a lot of work.)

### Time and condition conjunctions

Time conjunctions are used to indicate when something happens.

"Will" or "Would" or going to + infinitive are not used after time Conjunctions.

A comma is used when the time clause or the condition clause comes before the main clause.
A comma is used when we have a subordinate (dependent) clause followed by an independent clause. It is not used when we have an independent clause followed by a dependent clause.

**As soon as** I came home**,** I started packing.

dependent clause    **comma**    independent clause

I started packing as soon as I came home(no comma)

| TIME CLAUSES | CONDITION CLAUSES |
|---|---|
| after | on condition that |
| as long as | as long as |
| as soon as | provided/providing that |
| immediately (as soon as) | assuming that |
| | only if |
| before | suppose/supposing that |
| until | what if |
| by the time | |
| the moment | even if/though |
| the minute | if |
| the next time | unless |
| the sooner..the.. | in case |
| once | |
| until/till | |
| (ever) since | |
| when | |
| whenever | |
| while | |
| whilst (formal) | |

**After time and condition clauses we use past tenses to refer to the past:**

I took an umbrella **in case it rained.**

**Immediately** she had left the building, there was an explosion.(As soon as she left the building,...)

**Ever since Anna came** back from the island, she has been miserable.

We are not required to use past perfect after "after" and "before" for the action that happened first, since the order of events is clearly indicated by the conjunctions.

The postman came **after I ( had )left.**

She went to bed **before I (had) come home**.

We do, however, use **past perfect after "when" to indicate that something happened before something else.**

**When** I came home, **she had gone** to bed.

**"when"⮕time conjunction**
**"when"+ present tenses⮕for the present and future**

When I see him, I will give him my number

> **"when + simple past ⮕ for the past**

When I saw him the other day, I gave him my number.

> **"When" used as a question word can be followed by future tenses.**
> **When ⮕ question word + will/would/going to**

When will you see him?

When are you going to come home?

> **"When"** after the words **"I don't know"**, can be followed by future tenses.

**I don't know when** I will see you again.

> **"While"** and **"as"** are followed by continuous tenses and they are used to emphasize the **duration of an action.**

She sneaked in the auditorium **while** the professeur **was giving** a lecture.

**While I was taking** a shower, I heard you come in.

You interrupted me **when I was talking.**

**You were knocking** on the door **while I was taking** a shower.

**While** can also be used to describe **two actions happening at the same time.**

**While** the professeur **was giving** a lecture, the students were taking notes.

The students were taking notes **while** the professor **was giving a lecture.**

**While I'm talking** to you, **you're reading** the newspaper.

**"When"** can also be used to describe **two actions happening at the same time.**

**When I'm talking** to you, **you're reading** the newspaper.

**While I was working, you were sleeping.**

**"When" + simple past** is also used to describe **a shorter action that interrupted a longer one.**

**I was taking** a shower **when the telephone rang.**

**By/Until**
**Until= (not after)** Until emphasises **how long something continuous before it is completed at a certain point.**

You have **until** Friday to hand in your composition.(=You can't hand it in after Friday, but you have plenty of time until then.)

Don't buy me that shirt I told you I liked **until** I give you the money.(=Don't buy it before I give you the money.)

**"By"(=not after )Something will happen before a certain point. "By" gives a dead line.**

You have to hand in your composition **by Friday.**(=You can't hand it in after Friday)

I will give you the money **by Friday.** (=I won't give you the money after Friday)

I want you to be here **by** Friday.(=Make sure you come before Friday.)

## UNREAL PAST TENSES AND THE SUBJUNCTIVE

### Unreal past (past subjunctive)

The Unreal past is used to express wishes, imaginary situations, commands regrets or polite requests in the present, past or future.

The unreal past (past subjunctive) is used after **wish, if only, it's high time, it's about time, would rather, would sooner, suppose, as if, although**.

The subjunctive **(were in all persons) is used to express wishes in the present.** If you wish something had been different in the past you use a past perfect tense.

The expression **it's time, it's about time, it's high time** is not used with past perfect as it refers to the present.

I wish she **weren't** so absolute about everything.

I wish she **weren't** such a domineering mother. ( the use of "were" instead of "was" is more formal)

I wish she **wasn't** such a domineering mother. ( the use of "was" instead of "were" is more informal)

I wish he **were** more cooperative.

I would rather we **went** to Mykonos by plane.

You're acting **as if something terrible happened** to you.

I wish you **had come** with us yesterday. We had so much fun.

If only you **had been** there to see the expression on his face.

## Unreal Past Tenses with "Wish" = "If only"

| | | |
|---|---|---|
| **Wish/if only+ Simple Past** | ⮑**regret about a PRESENT situation** | (Chris isn't here) I wish he was/were. |
| Wish/if only + Past Continuous | ⮑regret about a **PRESENT situation** | I wish I was/were coming. (=I'm not coming) |
| **Wish/if only + Past Perfect** | ⮑regret about a **PAST situation** | I wish I had gone to the party.(=Why didn't I go?) |
| Wish/if only + Past Perfect Continuous | ⮑regret about a **PAST situation** | I wish I had been sleeping.(Why wasn't I sleeping?) |
| **Wish / if only +Could/Would** | ⮑ **a wish for the FUTURE** | I wish you would come with me. (=Why don't you come with me?) |
| For future reference we can also use the verb "hope" +simple present or simple future. | | I hope (that) he comes /will come. |
| **Wish / if only + Could/ Would** | ⮑**a strong wish for the PRESENT** | I wish he would call me. (=Why doesn't he call?) |
| For a strong wish in the present or future we can also use the verb "hope" +simple present or simple future. | | I hope (that) he calls/ will call me. |
| Wish/if only + Could/ Would | ⮑annoyance in the present | I wish you would stop talking. (=Why are you always talking?) |
| | | I wish you wouldn't lie all the time. (=Why are you always lying?) |
| | | I wish you would stop lying |

We can't use would when we have the same subject with " wish."
We use **"could" instead of "would"** (He......he, We......we etc.):

☒ **I** wish **I** would go with you

☑ **I** wish **I could** go with you

☒ **He** wishes **he** would concentrate

☑ **He** wishes **he could** concentrate

We can't use would when we have the same subject with **"If only I…"** We use **"could" instead of "would."**

**If only=I wish**

☒ If only I would go with you

☑ If only I **could** go with you

With **"wish"** and **"if only"** we usually use **"were"** instead of "was" especially in writing.

**If only/ she were** here

**I wish /If only you were** more confident

More about **"wish"** and **"hope":**

**Wish +full infinitive**

I wish to talk to you (= I want to talk to you)

**Wish + object pronoun+noun**

I wish you a Merry Christmas

I wish you happiness

**Wish someone the best**

I wish you the best (of everything)

**Hope +full infinitive**

I hope to talk to you later(= I would like to talk to you later)

**Hope+ clause**

I hope you come to my party.(=I would like you to come to my party)

**would rather/would sooner, had better**

**We'd better tell** her the truth

(=We should tell her the truth)

**I would rather/would sooner watch** a comedy

(=I prefer to watch a comedy)

## Unreal past tenses with: would rather (would sooner)

| When we have would rather/would sooner with 1 subject we use bare infinitive for the **PRESENT+ FUTURE** | |
|---|---|
| **I would rather do something**<br>   bare infinitive | **I would rather feed the dog.**<br>   **not feed the dog**<br>   (negative) |
| When we have would rather/would sooner **with 1 subject** we use **perfect infinitive** for the **PAST** | |
| **I would rather have done something**<br>   perfect infinitive | **I would rather have gone to the party.**<br>   **not have gone to the party**<br>   (negative) |
| When we have **would rather/would sooner/would sooner** with 2 subjects we use simple past for the PRESENT+FUTURE to show that we would like someone to do something for us. | |
| **I would rather you did something something**<br>   **simple past** (unreal past) | **I would rather you stopped talking.**<br>**I would rather you didn't make me feel bad.** (negative)<br>**I would rather you came with us tomorrow.** |
| When we have **would rather/would sooner** with 2 subjects we use **past perfect for the PAST** to show that we wish we had done or that we had not done something. | |
| **I would rather you had done something**<br>**past perfect** (unreal past) | **I would rather you had told me the truth.**<br>**I would rather you hadn't lied to me.** (negative) |
| **Also:It would have been better if+ past perfect:** | It would have been better if you had done something. |

## Unreal past tenses with: It's time

**It's time to do sth**
**for someone to do sth**
**someone did sth**

**It's time to go** to bed.

**It's time for you to go** to bed.

**It's time you went** to bed.(Unreal simple past is used to talk about a present situation.)

*Note:* only the **unreal simple past** is used **after it's time** when there is a change of subject
In some cases we use simple past to talk about a present situation. We call that "unreal past":

**It's time you went** to bed.
**It's time he left.**
**It's time they came.**

*Note*: **Past perfect is not possible** because "it's time" or "it's about/high time" refer to a present situation.

**It's high/about time someone did sth**

✗ **Its about/high time to go** to bed.

✗ **It's about/high time** for you to go to bed.

✓**It's high/about time you went** to bed. It's getting late.

*Note:* only the unreal simple past is used after it's high/about time:

128

## As if/as though

We use unreal **Past simple** p to talk **about imaginary actions in the present** and **past perfect** to talk about **imaginary or unreal actions and situations in the past.**

You act **as if/though I didn't inform** you. (=I might not have)

You act **as if you were** the boss.(=I don't think you are)

You looked **as if you had won** the lottery.(=I don't think you did) (when the action of the as if clause refers to an action before the action of the main clause)

**Note: Present and Perfect tenses** can be used **after as if/though to express real situations:**

The house looks **as if it has been broken into.**(=it probably has)

You act **as if you are** the boss.(=it is possible that you are)

(see page 103-104 for more on "as if")

## PRESENT SUBJUNCTIVE

The subjunctive is used to express ideas that are not facts. It is used in very formal language, in poetry and in reported speech. There are some verbs, nouns adjectives and expressions that require: **a)** the use of a **that clause with a bare infinitive (subjunctive verb)** **or: b)** instead of a subjunctive verb **should +bare infinitive:**

I    suggest (that) he  see a doctor
   ( that clause  +  subject  + bare infinitive)

I     suggest(that) he     should  see a doctor.
( that clause  +  subject  + should + bare infinitive)

Object pronouns (me, you, him, her, it, us, you, them are not used with the subjunctive:

❌ **I suggest** him to see a doctor.

✅ **I suggest** (that) he see a doctor.

✅ **I suggest** (that) he sees a doctor.(This is also possible in very informal English.)

**Note:** The subjunctive is used regardless of the time reference. **It is used to talk about present, past and future:**

I suggested **that he be told** immediately.(I advised you, him, her, them to tell him immediately.)

I suggest **that she leave** first thing in the morning. (I advised her to leave first thing in the morning.)

The use of a **Present tense is possible in informal English only if the introductory verb is in the present**:

☑ I **recommend** that he **tries/ try** this new restaurant in town. (since the subjunctive verb "recommend" is in the present, a present tense is possible)

☒ I **recommended** that he ~~tries~~ this new restaurant in town.

☑ I **recommend** that he **try/should try** this new restaurant in town.

> The Subjunctive is used more in American English than in British English. The British use more the should + bare infinitive construction.

**Although simple past can also be used when the introductory verb is in the past, the bare infinitive or the should construction is recommended:**

☑ I **recommended** that he **tried** this new restaurant in town.(less common)

☑ I **recommended** that he **try** this new restaurant in town.

☑ I **recommended** that he **should try** this new restaurant in town.

☒ I **recommend** that he **tried** this new restaurant.

The Present subjunctive is used to express urgency, suggestions, or plans. This is a list of some of the verbs used with the subjunctive:

| | | |
|---|---|---|
| **advise** | agree | **ask** |
| **beg** | hope | **(would) prefer** |
| **petition** | suggest | recommend |
| **propose** | require | **request** |
| **demand** | command | **order** |
| **insist** | urge | **desire** |
| **whisper** | vote etc | |

☑ The judge **recommended** that he **serve** 5 years in prison.

☑ The judge **recommended** that he should **serve** 5 years in prison.

☑ The judge recommended **that he should not be given** a harsh punishment. (negative)

☑ The judge recommended **that he not be given** a harsh punishment.( negative )

☑ I suggest **that we not rush** into anything.

☑ It was suggested **that we look** into the matter.

☑ It was suggested **that he not resign.**

132

This is a list of some of the **nouns** used with the subjunctive:

| suggestion | recommendation | **proposal** |
|---|---|---|
| **requirement** | demand | **insistence** |
| **necessity** | importance | **request** |
| **wish** | preference | |

He accepted my request **that I be informed** as soon as there was some news.

My proposal **that I be given** the position of assistant manager was turned down.

Your insistence **that he stay** is not very polite.

This is a list of some of the **adjectives** and **expressions** used with the subjunctive:

| **it is important** | it is vital | **it is essential** |
|---|---|---|
| **it is necessary** | it is crucial | **it is urgent** |
| **it is imperative** | it is mandatory | **it is fundamental** |
| **it is best** | it is of vital importance | **it is of paramount importance** |

It is crucial **that he be** admitted to the hospital.

It is necessary **that we leave** immediately.

It is imperative **that she adopt** a healthier life style.

It is of vital importance **that the papers be** signed as soon as possible.

**Notes:** Past tenses and modals (will, can, may, should, ought to) should not be used, however, simple past can sometimes be used when the subjunctive verb is in a past tense:

☑ I suggested **that she see** a doctor.

☑ I suggested **that she should see** a doctor.

☑ I suggested that she saw a doctor.(less common)

☒ I suggest that she saw a doctor.

☑ It was urgent that she go to the hospital.

☑ It was urgent that she went to the hospital.(less common)

☒ It is urgent that she went to the hospital.

☑ It is urgent that she go to the hospital.

☑ It is urgent that she goes to the hospital.

☑ It is necessary **that the passengers be informed** of the delay.

☑ It is necessary **that the passengers should be informed** of the delay.

☑ It is necessary that the passengers **are informed** of the delay. (less common)

☒ It is necessary that the passengers will be informed of the delay.(modals are not used)

### after some expressions:

Heaven forbid **(=you hope that something will not happen)(not very polite)**
come what may (=**no matter what happens**)
so be it
suffice it to say**( even though you could say more, what you say is enough to get your message across.)**
Long live the Queen
God bless America
far be it from me
may peace be with you
May he rest in peace
until death do us part
if need be( =**if it's necessary**)
truth be told
rest in peace

rest his soul
may the best man win
may God bless you
God willing
**I will not abandon you** come what may. (=**no matter what happens**)
May his soul rest in peace.
So be it.

### after "whether, whatever, if, etc" :

Whether **he (should) be** here or not, we're proceeding with the formalities. (=whether he is here or not, we're .....)

Whatever **he (should) decide to do,** we will support him. (=whatever **he decides to do,** we.....)

If he **(should) be told/is told** the truth, I'm sure he will appreciate it.

**If need be,** we'll work over time. (=if it is necessary, we'll...)

**If that be** the case, I'll try to talk to him.(=if that is the case, I'll ......)

The past subjunctive is used after wish, If only, It's high/about/time, would rather, would sooner, suppose, as if/ as though:
**(see page 123 for more on the past subjunctive)**

# INVERSIONS

**Inversion=auxiliary verb +subject +main verb**

**The inversion is used:**

### to form questions

**Do you know** the deadline for the applications?

**How old are you?**

**Are you ready** to leave?

### with so/neither/nor to express agreement or disagreement

I have been to many countries and **so have you.**

You like working out and **so do we.**

I didn't sleep and **neither/nor did Ann.**

I won't approve and **neither/nor will your father.**

### with **such/so/to such a degree** in the beginning of a sentence

**So beautifully did he sing** that the audience wouldn't stop clapping.
(=He sang so beautifully that the audience wouldn't stop clapping.)

**Such a beautiful day was it** that we decided to spend the day at the beach.
(=It was such a beautiful day that we decided to spend the day at the beach.)

**So beautiful a day was** it that we decided to spend the day at the beach.
(=It was so beautiful a day that we decided to spend the day at the beach.)

## Inverted conditional sentences

**with conditionals: Should I ... (Type 1), Were I...( Type 2), Had I...(Type 3)**

**Should you meet** the head of the department, would you be so kind as to introduce him to me?
( =If you should meet.../ if you meet...)

**Were I** in your place, I would not turn down such an offer.
(=If I were in your place...)

**Had I known** what the requirements for the position were, I would have been more prepared
( =If I had known....**)**

**with adverbs and adverbial expressions** when they are placed **first in the sentence:**

| |
|---|
| Hardly/Scarcely/Barely...when |
| No sooner... than |
| Hardly ever |
| Never |
| Never before |
| Not only...but also |
| Nowhere |
| Not once |
| On no occasion/condition/account + auxiliary verb+ subject + verb |
| At no time |
| In no way |
| In/Under no circumstances |
| Rarely/seldom |
| Only then |
| Little |
| Many a time (can be followed by an inversion) |
| How many times (usually followed by an inversion) |
| Only if Not until/till |
| Only when Not since |
| Only by |
| Only after |

**No sooner** had the teacher entered the classroom **than** the students started talking.
(=As soon as the teacher entered the classroom, the students started talking.**)**


**Hardly/Scarcely/Barely** had I gone outside **when** it started raining.
(=As soon as I went outside, it started raining.)


**Never before** have I seen anyone so selfish.
(=I have never seen anyone so selfish before.)


**On no occasion/under no circumstances/on no account** should you repeat what you heard here today.
(=You should not repeat what you heard here today under any circumstances.)


**Seldom** do I go out anymore.
(=I seldom go out anymore.)

**Little** did I know what he was planning on doing with the money he borrowed.
(= I didn't know/suspect what he was planning on doing with the money he borrowed.)

**Only then** did I realize that it was a lost cause.
(=I realized then that it was a lost cause.)

**Many a time** have I warned you about the risks involved in this job.
(=I have warned you many times about the risks involved in this job.)

**How many times** have I told you not to trust this person?
(=I have told you many times not to trust this person, haven't I?)

**At no time/Never** did I intend to tell him.
(= I never intended to tell him.)

**Note:** After the following, **the inversion takes place in the main clau**se and not in the clause following the phrase.
**(It is not the first verb that is inverted.)**

| |
|---|
| **Only if/Not until/till** |
| **Only when/Not since** |
| **Only by** |
| **Only after** |
| **Only before** |

**Only when** the children had finished their breakfast **were they given** permission to go out and play. (=The children were given permission to go out and play only when they had finished their breakfast.)

**Only if** you abide by his laws **are you considered** a trustworthy friend.(=You are considered a true friend only if you abide by his laws.)

**Only by** working hard **will you be able** to accomplish your goal.(=If you work hard, you will be able to accomplish your goal.)

| |
|---|
| with adverbs of place +verbs that indicate movement ( Here,.. There,.. ) (literary inversions) |

**There goes** my money.

**Here comes** Mary.

**Out go** the children.

*Note:* If the subject of the sentence is a subject pronoun, we cannot have an inversion

- ❌ ~~There goes~~ ~~it~~
- ❌ ~~Here comes~~ ~~she~~
- ❌ ~~Out go~~ ~~they~~
- ❌ ~~Off goes~~ ~~he~~
- ✓ There it goes
- ✓ Here she comes
- ✓ Out they go
- ✓ Off he goes

**with adverbs of time (First, then, Finally + be or verb of movement ( go, come, stand,…) ( literary inversions)**

**First came** the groom and **then arrived** the bride.

**with "as"** ( something happens in the same way)

I have always supported you, **as have** all the family.

Anthony decided to visit me on my birthday, **as** did all my friends

**when we are making wishes**

**May you find** the happiness that you deserve.

**May he rest** in peace.

**with exclamations**

**Wasn't it** a nice gesture!

**Isn't it** a great opportunity!

## PASSIVE VOICE

The passive is perhaps more common in English than in any other language. It should, however, be used with caution to avoid using unnatural English.
In passive voice one is usually not interested in who performed the action but in the action itself:

Active voice ⇒ **The workers** are building **a garage.**

Passive voice ⇒ **A garage is being built.**

In passive voice:

a) the **object** in active voice **becomes the subject** of the sentence in passive voice.

b) we put **the verb to be** in **the same tense as the tense of the main verb** in active.

c) we add **the past participle of the main verb.**

d **The agent**, however, many times not necessary **is expressed with(by).**

Active voice ⇒ **The workers**      **built**      **a garage.**
                   subject     + s. past     + object

Passive voice ⇒ **A garage**    **was built**    **by the workers.**
                    subject    + past participle   +agent

**"By" is omitted** when the subject is not necessary, important unknown or obvious:

My hair has been dyed. (One is not interested in who dyed it.)

The truth has been told. (It is not important who told the truth.)

His injury has been taken care of. (It's obvious that the doctors took care of it.)

The kids were told to turn off the light. ( it is not important who told them to turn off the lights)

Experiments are conducted in search of a cure for Aids. ( It is obvious that scientists are conducting the experiments.)

I was born in Athens, Greece. (It is obvious who gave birth to me.)


## The passive is usually used:

in more formal and spoken English

The players **must be informed** of the cancellation of the game. (passive)(formal)

The referee **must inform** the players of the cancellation of the game. (active)(informal)

in newspaper headlines, newspaper reports, academic and scientific writing

The robbers **were caught** at dawn....

in informal English with **get+ past participle**

Nicky **got punished** for lying to her mum. (She was punished.)

Some students **got caught** cheating on the test.(They were caught.)

to announce an accident with **get+past participle**

The athlete **got his knee injured**. (He injured his knee.)

I **got my finger cut.** (I injured my finger.)

More on Passive voice

## The passive with two objects

When we have two objects, a personal indirect object and a noun direct object, we usually change the personal indirect object into a subject pronoun, and place it at the beginning of the sentence to form the passive:

The cashier gave **me** a refund. ⊃active

**I** was given a refund by the cashier. ⊃passive

**The noun direct object** can also be used at the beginning of the sentence to form the passive for emphasis on that action:

The cashier gave me **a refund**. ⊃active

**A refund** was given to me by the cashier. ⊃ passive

### Let/allow

The verb **let** becomes **allow** in passive voice:

| Active | Passive |
|---|---|
| The police **let** the petty criminal **go**. | The petty criminal **was allowed to go.** |

### Make/see/help

The verbs **make, see, help, hear +bare infinitive in active** voice become **make, see, help, hear+ full infinitive in passive** voice:

| Active voice | Passive voice |
|---|---|
| **My boss made me work** over time. | **I was made to work** over time. |
| **Helen helped Maria do** her homework. | Maria **was helped to do** her homework. |
| **I saw him leave** the room. | He **was seen to leave** the room. |

Verbs which are followed by a preposition carry the **preposition right after the verb** in passive voice:

| Active voice | Passive voice |
|---|---|
| **I am looking** into the matter. | **The matter is being looked into.** |

### Something needs doing/Something needs to be done

The verbs **need/require/want/deserve** convey a passive meaning:

My hair **needs trimming.**
My hair **needs to be trimmed.**
The house **needs doing up.**
The house **needs to be done up.**
He **deserves praising for his work.**
He deserves **to be praised for his work.**
Your speech **requires some touching up.**
Your speech **requires to be touched up.**

## With/By

> Using **"with"** and **"by"** in passive voice. **"By"** is used **for the person** who or what performs the action, and **"with"** is used **for the object** used to perform the action:

I was informed **by** my professor that the class was cancelled.

Many people were killed **by** the avalanche.

He was shot **with** a shot gun.

He was stabbed **with** a knife.

### Stative verbs and the passive

> **Action verbs** express **what a person does**.
> **Stative verbs** express **states which continue over a period of time,** rather than actions and a lot of them are not usually used in passive voice. These are a few of the stative verbs that are very rarely used in passive voice:

| | | | |
|---|---|---|---|
| **have** | dislike | **matter** | appear |
| **own** | fear | **deserve** | seem |
| **possess (have)** | fear | **be** | fit |
| **belong to** | please | **cost** | consist of |
| **contain** | wish | **look** | owe |
| **smell** | taste | **sense** | |

☑ I have a really nice house.

☒ A really nice house is had by me.

☑ You deserve this award.

☒ This award is deserved by you.

**(for more on stative verbs see page 163)**

> When the verb **"possess"** is used in passive it has another meaning:

They possess a lot of wealth. ⇒ correct

A lot of wealth is possessed by them. ⇒ wrong

      **but**

He was possessed with fear. (=he was really scared) ⇒ correct

The film is about a man who is possessed.
(=he was controlled/influenced by Satan) ⇒ correct


> **The following are some of the most common stative verbs which can be used in passive:**

| | | | |
|---|---|---|---|
| **include** | know | **impress** | envy |
| **satisfy** | imagine | **include** | forget |
| **surprise** | recognize | **admire** | love, |
| **want** | suppose | **adore** | hate |
| **think** | understand | **astonish** | prefer |
| **believe** | remember | **envy** | |

**He is thought to have been** kidnapped.

This room **needs to be cleaned / cleaning.**

**We were surprised** to see you.

**The meals are included** in the price.

**I was so satisfied** by the meal you prepared for us.

**He is believed** to be a thief.

**He was loved** by everyone.

**I was astonished** by her disguise.

**You are not supposed to be** late for dinner.

> Unfortunately, there are no rules concerning when or not to use stative verbs in passive. The best way to learn them is by experience. I would strongly advise you to read as much as possible so as to acquire experience in using the language.

**Most students hate taking exams.**

✗ Exams are hated by students.

✓ You will be hated by everyone.

**I remember locking the door.**

✗ The door is remembered

✓ He will be remembered. (= we / they will not forget him)

**The prices do not include meals.**

✓ Meals are not included in the prices.

## Tenses of passive voice

| Active voice | Passive voice |
|---|---|
| The scientist **conducts** experiments. | Experiments **are** conducted (by the scientist.) |
| The **scientist is conducting** experiments. | Experiments **are being** conducted. |
| The scientist **has conducted** experiments. | Experiments **have been** conducted. |
| The scientist **has been conducting** experiments. | ----------------------------------- |
| The scientist **conducted** experiments. | Experiments **were** conducted. |
| The scientist **was conducting** experiments. | Experiments **were being** conducted. |
| The scientist **had conducted** experiments. | Experiments **had been** conducted. |
| The scientist **had been conducting** experiments. | ----------------------------------- |
| The scientist **will conduct** experiments. | Experiments will be conducted. |
| The scientist **will be conducting** experiments. | ----------------------------------- |
| The scientist **will have conducted** experiments. | Experiments **will have been** conducted. |
| The scientist **will have been conducting** experiments. | ----------------------------------- |
| The scientist **is going to conduct** experiments. | Experiments **are going to be** conducted. |
| The scientist **might/may/can/should** conduct experiments. | Experiments **might/may/can/should be** conducted. |

We **do not use passive constructions** for present perfect continuous, past perfect continuous, future continuous and future perfect continuous.

## Infinitives and gerunds in the passive

|  | Active | Passive |
|---|---|---|
| **Present infinitive:** | **to inform**<br>I must inform everyone. | **to be informed**<br>Everyone must be informed. |
| **Perfect infinitive:** | **to have informed**<br>They should have informed us. | **to have been informed**<br>We should have been informed. |
| **Present gerund:** | **informing**<br>I forgot your informing us. | **being informed**<br>I forgot being informed. |
| **Perfect gerund:** | **having informed**<br>I forgot your having informed us. | **having been informed**<br>I forgot having been informed. |

### Passive infinitives

When the verbs **believe, claim, supposed to, think, reported, expect, know, say** are used to express what people, in general, think or how they feel about something we use either:
a) **the personal passive construction** or b) **the impersonal passive construction "it":**

They **think** that he **is/will be** a nice person. ⮕ active voice

a) He **is thought** to be a nice person. ⮕ personal passive construction

⬇

**Present infinitive**

b) **It is thought** that he is a nice person. ⮕ impersonal passive construction

People **believed** that **he's hiding/will be hiding/** somewhere.

a) He **was** believed **to be hiding** somewhere.

         ⇩

      **Present continuous infinitive**

b) It **was believed** that he's hiding somewhere.


**They know** that we **were/have been/ had been** associates.

a) **We are known to have been** associates.

         ⇩

       **Perfect infinitive**

b) **It is known** that we were associates.


**They suppose** that he **was working/has been working/had been working hard.**

a) **He is supposed to have been working** hard.

         ⇩

     **Perfect continuous infinitive**

b) **It is supposed** that he was working hard.

## Tenses corresponding with the Infinitives

| | |
|---|---|
| They think that **he's** a nice man.  *present simple* ➲ | He is thought **to be** a nice man.  *present infinitive* |
| They believe that **he's hiding** somewhere.  *present continuous* ➲ | He is believed **to be hiding** somewhere.  *present continuous infinitive* |
| They claim that **she worked/has worked/ had worked hard.**  *simple past, present perfect, past perfect* ➲ | She is believed **to have worked** hard.  **Perfect infinitive** |
| They say that **they were studying/have been studying/ had been studying hard.** *past continuous, present perfect continuous, past perfect continuous* ➲ | They are said **to have been studying** hard.  *perfect continuous infinitive* |

## CAUSITIVE

The causative expresses an action performed by **someone else.** Someone else does something for you.

**Passive causative form:** There is no agent in the passive form.

### Have/get something done
### Subject+Have/get (in the appropriate tense) + noun+the past participle of the verb)

Once every two months the hairdresser trims my hair.

Once every two months **I have my hair trimmed.** ⊃causitive

(have +noun +past participle)


**Get is a more informal construction:**

Once every two months **I get my hair trimmed.** ⊃ **more informal causative**

( get +noun +past participle)


**The causative is also used to state that somebody does something to you:**

I had my house broken into. (=Somebody broke into my house.)

I had my car crashed. (=Somebody crashed my car.)

**Active causative form:** This construction is usually used when giving instructions. There is an agent in the active form.

> **Have someone do something (=ask someone to do something)**
>
> **Get someone to do something ( =convince someone to do something)**

Once every two months I **have the hairdresser trim** my hair.

**Get is a more informal construction than have:**

Once every two months I **get the hairdresser to trim** my hair.

I **got my mum to clean** my room.

## Tenses of causative (passive causative)
### Have/get something done

| Simple present: | I have/get my hair trimmed. |
|---|---|
| Present continuous : | I'm having/getting my hair trimmed. |
| Present perfect : | I have had/ gotten my hair trimmed. |
| Present perfect continuous: | I have been having /getting my hair trimmed. |
| Simple past: | I had/got my hair cut. |
| Past perfect: | I hadhad /had gotten my hair trimmed. |
| Past perfect continuous: | I had been having/getting my hair trimmed. |
| Past continuous: | I was having/getting my hair cut. |
| Simple future: | I will have/get my hair trimmed. |
| Future continuous: | I will be having/getting my hair trimmed. |
| Future perfect: | I will have had/gotten my hair trimmed. |
| Future perfect continuous: | I will have been having/getting my hair trimmed. |
| Going to: | I am going to have/get my hair trimmed. |
| Modals: | I can, may, might, etc have/get my hair trimmed. |

## Have someone doing something (=succeed in helping someone do something)

I will **have you speaking** English in no time.(=I will succeed in teaching you how to speak English.)

Tenses of causative **(active causative)**
Have someone do something

| | |
|---|---|
| **Simple present:** | I have my hairdresser trim my hair. |
| **Present continuous:** | I'm having my hairdresser trim my hair. |
| **Present perfect :** | I have had my hairdresser trim my hair |
| **Present perfect continuous:** | I have been having my hairdresser trim my hair. |
| **Simple past:** | I had my hairdresser trim my hair. |
| **Past continuous:** | I was having my hairdresser trim my hair. |
| **Past perfect:** | I had had my hairdresser trim my hair. |
| **Past perfect continuous:** | I had been having my hairdresser trim my hair. |
| **Simple future:** | I will have my hairdresser trim my hair. |
| **Future continuous:** | I will be having my hairdresser trim my hair. |
| **Future perfect:** | I will have had my hairdresser trim my hair. |
| **Future perfect continuous:** | I will have been having my hairdresser trim my hair. |
| **Going to:** | I am going to have my hairdresser trim my hair. |
| **Modals:** | I may/might/etc have my hairdresser trim my hair. |

## Get someone to do something

| | |
|---|---|
| **Simple present:** | I get the hairdresser to trim my hair. |
| **Present continuous:** | I'm getting the hairdresser to trim my hair. |
| **Present perfect:** | I have gotten my hairdresser to trim my hair. |
| **Present perfect continuous:** | I have been getting my hairdresser to trim my hair. |
| **Simple past:** | I got my hairdresser to trim my hair. |
| **Past continuous:** | I was getting my hairdresser to trim my hair. |
| **Past perfect:** | I had got my hairdresser to trim my hair. |
| **Past perfect continuous:** | I had been getting my hairdresser to trim my hair. |
| **Simple future:** | I will get my hairdresser to trim my hair. |
| **Future continuous:** | I will be getting my hairdresser to trim my hair. |
| **Future perfect:** | I will have gotten my hairdresser to trim my hair. |
| **Future perfect continuous:** | I will have been getting my hairdresser to trim my hair. |
| **Going to+infinitive:** | I am going to get my hairdresser to trim my hair. |
| **Modal+bare infinitive:** | I can/may/might/etc get my hairdresser to trim my hair. |

## PRESENT TENSES
### Simple present
**STRUCTURE**

In the third person singular of regular verbs: **verb +s/es**

My mother read**s** the paper every day.

| Affirmative | Interrogative | Negative | Short Form |
|---|---|---|---|
| **I dream** | **Do I** dream? | **I do not** dream | **I don't** dream |
| **You dream** | Do you dream? | You do not dream | You don't dream |
| **He/she/it dreams** | Does he/she/it dream? | He/she/it does not dream | He/she/it doesn't dream |
| **We dream** | Do we dream? | We do not dream | We don't dream |
| **You dream** | Do you dream? | You do not dream | You don't dream |
| **They dream** | Do they dream? | They do not dream | They don't dream |

**The verb have is irregular in the third person singular:**
I, you, we, you, they **have**/ he, she, it **has**

I always **have** coffee in the morning.

He always **has** supper at six o'clock.

| Affirmative | Short form | Negative | Short form | Interrogative |
|---|---|---|---|---|
| **I have** | I've | **I do not have** | I don't have | **Do I have?** |
| **You have** | You've | **You do not have** | You don't have | **Do you have?** |
| **He/she/it** has | He's/she's/it's | **He/she/it does not have** | He/she/it doesn't have | **Does he/she/it have?** |
| **We have** | We've | **We do not have** | We don't have | **Do we have?** |
| **You have** | You've | **You do not have** | You don't have | **Do you have?** |
| **They have** | They've | **They do not have** | They don't have | **Do they have?** |

**The verb "be" is irregular and the interrogative and negative is formed with the same verb:**

**Gus is a very gifted kid.**

**Helen is not here today.**

**Is john here?**

| Affirmative | Short Form | Negative | Short Form | Interrogative |
|---|---|---|---|---|
| **I am** | I'm | **I am not** | I'm not | **Am I?** |
| **You are** | You're | **You are not** | You're not | **Are you?** |
| **He/she/it is** | He/she/it's | **He/she/it is not** | He's/she's/it's not or He/she/it isn't | **Is he/she/it?** |
| **We are** | We're | **We are not** | We're not or We aren't | **Are we?** |
| **You are** | You're | **You are not** | You're not or You aren't | **Are you?** |
| **They are** | They're | **They are not** | They're not or They aren't | **Are they?** |

If a verb ends in **ss, z, sh, ch, o** we use **"es"** instead of "s" in the third person singular:

She tea**ch**es Chinese.

He always mi**ss**es the bus, and he has to walk to school.

A detective sear**ch**es for clues.

The color of your sweater mat**ch**es your dress.

He always wakes up late and then ru**sh**es off to work.

She drops the children off to school and then g**o**es to work.

**If a verb ends in consonant+y we change the "y" to an "i" and add "es":**

Try ⮕ He always tri**es** to be on time.

Stu**dy** ⮕ She stud**ies** very hard.

**Modal verbs do not take an "s" in the third person singular:**

She **can't** be serious. She **must** be joking.

He **should** be home soon.

**In interrogative, negative sentences and short answers of regular verbs we use: do/does**

-**Do** you know why they're late?

-No, **I don't.**

-**Does** she speak English?

-Yes, **she does.**

**Short forms of all verbs in the negative: don't/doesn't**

I **don't** like tennis.

My daughter **doesn't have a computer.**

I **dont** approve of smoking.

My teen-age daughter **doesn't have any confidence in herself.**

**Short forms of the verb "to be": I'm, you're, he's, she's, it's, we're, you're, they're**

Anthony is a good kid, but **he's** always late for class.

Helen is very diligent. **She's** efficient in everything she does.

Short answers of all verbs in the present: **I, you, we, they do/don't/ She, he, it does/doesn't**

Do you know her? Yes, **I do.** No, **I don't.**

Does she know us? Yes, **She does.** No, **she doesn't.**

Short answers of the verb "to be" in the present: **I am, you, we, they are/ he, she, it is**
**I am not, you, we, they are not, he, she, it, is not**

Are you happy? Yes, **I am.** No, **I am not.**

Yes, **we are.** No, **we are not.**

Is she arrogant? Yes, **she is.** No, **she is not.**

**USE**
We use simple present for:

**present habits**

I have breakfast at 7:00 a.m.

**repeated actions usually with frequency adverbs (usually, often, frequently, rarely, seldom, etc)**

The whole family **always has** lunch together on Sundays.

**general truths**

**It rarely snows** in Southern Greece.

**laws of nature**

**The sun sets** in the west.

### timetables and schedules in the near future

Our dancing class **begins at 6:00 p.m.**

The plane **takes off at 7:00 p.m.**

### states with STATIVE VERBS

**I love** chocolate.

**I hate** hypocrites.

### sports commentaries and reviews of novels, film, plays, etc

**Beckham scores** and the **audience scream** with joy.

### narrations and jokes even when we are talking about the past

Mark Twain's novel Tom Sawyer and Huckleberry Finn is set in St. Petersburg, Missouri, a small village on the banks of the Mississippi River in the mid-1800s.

### newspaper headlines

Snow storm stops traffic.

### after "if", "when", and "after" to talk about the future

**If you finish** work early, meet me for lunch.

**When I see** him, I will let him in on what happened.

> **Frequency adverbs and time expressions used with simple present:**
> (every day/week/month/year/Monday/Tuesday etc), (always, often, usually, sometimes, never, seldom, rarely), (once a day/ week/ month/ year), (twice a day/ week/ month), (on Mondays/ Tuesdays, etc.)

**Action verbs** express **what a person does**. **State verbs** express **states which continue over a period of time**, rather than actions and here is a list of the most frequently used stative verbs:

| Senses | hear, see, smell, taste, feel, sound |
|---|---|
| Possession | have, own, want, contain, belong to |
| Emotions | like, love, enjoy hate, dislike, want, need, prefer, hope, wish, feel, forgive |
| Opinion | think, believe, suppose, agree, understand, seem |
| Measurement | weigh, cost, measure, equal |
| Mental states | know, remember, forget, mean, look(appear), mind |
| Other stative verbs | decide, resemble, tend, conclude, perceive, appreciate, recognize, be(exist), etc |

When the following stative verbs are used in progressive (continuous) tenses, they have a different meaning than when they are used in non-progressive tenses:

| Non-progressive | Progressive(continuous) |
|---|---|
| "**have**" with the meaning of possession | "**have**" enjoy one self |
| "**see**" look with the eyes | "**see**" meet or date sm |
| "**think**" believe | "**think**" someone's thoughts |
| "**feel**" describing someone's mood | "**feel**" touch |
| "**smell**" talking about how something smells | "**smell**" using one's nose to understand how something smells |
| "**be**" describing how you are | "**be**" behaving in a certain way |
| "**appear**" seem | "**appear**" give a performance, give a speech, etc |

# Present continuous
## Structure

| Affirmative | Short | Negative | Short | Interrogative |
|---|---|---|---|---|
| I am dreaming | I'm | I am not dreaming | I'm not | Am I dreaming? |
| You are dreaming | You're | You are not dreaming. | You're not | Are you dreaming? |
| He/she/it is dreaming | He's/she's | He/she/it is not dreaming | He's/she's/it's not | Is he/she/it dreaming? |
| We are dreaming | We're | We are not dreaming | We're not | Are we dreaming? |
| You are dreaming | You're | You are not dreaming | You're not | Are you dreaming? |
| They are dreaming | They're | They are not dreaming | They're not | Are they dreaming? |

## Structure

### no short forms in the interrogative

Are you playing?

### Use

We use present continuous, also called present progressive for:

### something happening now.(at present)

I'm talking to you.

The kids are studying right now.

Turn the television down. The kids are sleeping.

**longer actions in progress at the present moment(now),** but not necessarily happening at the moment of speaking(now)

I'm living in Athens.

Romy is studying to become a lawyer.

I'm still working on this grammar book.

**future plans and arrangements in the near future**

When are you coming home?

I'm working next week.

**repeated actions which are annoying to the speaker with always, forever, constantly**

You're always coming home late.

Helen is constantly complaining.

**Note:** Stative verbs are not usually used in continuous tenses because they are not action verbs.

**Expressions used with present continuous:**
Now, at the moment (of speaking,) look! listen!, right now, still, currently, today, tonight, this week, this month, tomorrow, on Monday, Tuesday, etc, next week.

## Present perfect
## Structure

| | | | |
|---|---|---|---|
| Affirmative: | Subject + | has/have + | past participle of the main verb |
| Negative | Subject + | has/have not + | past participle of the main verb |
| Interrogative | Have/has + | Subject + | past participle of the main verb |

I **have** always **loved** you.

I **have not been** to Egypt yet.

**Have you seen** Mary recently?

Most past participles end in -ed. There is a long list, however, of irregular past participles at the end of this book that must be learned by heart.

| Affirmative | Affirmative short | Negative | Negative short | Interrogative |
|---|---|---|---|---|
| I have loved | I've | I have not loved | I haven't | Have I loved? |
| You have loved | you've | You have not loved | You haven't | Have you loved? |
| He has loved | he's | He has not loved | He hasn't | Has he loved? |
| She has loved | She's | She has not loved | She hasn't | Has she loved? |
| It has loved | It's | It has not loved | It hasn't | Has it loved? |
| We have loved | We've | We have not loved | We haven't | Have we loved? |
| You have loved | You've | You have not loved | You haven't | Have you loved? |
| They have loved | They've | They have not loved | They haven't | Have they loved? |

Use

We use the present perfect :

for an action that happened at an **indefinite/unspecified time** in the past. We are not interested in when the action happened, but in what happened.

**I have told you** what she said.

**Have you ever ridden** a horse?

for an action that **happened in the past**, but **has an effect on the present**.

I **haven't seen my parents** for three years.
(=The last time I saw my parents was three years ago).

for an action that started in the past and is still going on.(often with **"for"/ "since"**)

**I have lived** in Greece for 27 years.
(=I came to Greece 27 years ago, and I'm still living here.)

for an action that was repeated several times in the past with emphasis on quantity. (usually with **twice/three times, etc/many/several times etc.**)

**I have seen** this musical **several times.**

**I have been** to Paris **three times.**

After **this is / it is / he is+ SUPERLATIVE + Present perfect:**

**This is the best** book (that) **I have ever read.**

**This is the most interesting** lecture **I have ever attended.**

after **it is / this is the first /second/last/only time+ Present Perfect:**

It is **the first time** I have (that) ever said that.

> **Time expressions and prepositional phrases used with interrogative and negative sentences:** for, since, how long, recently, lately, yet, just, never, ever, already, so far, up to now, today, this week/month/year, all day/week/morning, etc.

Have you seen John **recently**?

**How long** have you been studying English?

Have you called home **yet?**

We do not use the present perfect with definite time expressions such as yesterday, last week, two months ago, etc. We use simple past instead.

I **came** to Greece 30 years ago.

Present perfect and present perfect continuous are used interchangeably when talking about an action that started in the past, and continuous into the present with verbs of movement such as live, work, etc

I **have lived** in Greece since 1980.

I **have been living** in Greece since 1980.

Time expressions, usually come between has/have and the main verb. However, **yet** comes at the end of a sentence, **so far** comes at the beginning or end of a sentence, and **ever** is used in questions:

I have **never** been to Australia.

Have you been to Rome **yet?**

**So far** we have talked about present tenses.

We have talked about present tenses **so far**.

Have you **ever** been to Rome?

168

## Have gone to/have been to/have been in:

Helen **has gone to** Egypt.(She hasn't come back yet).

Helen **has been to** Egypt.(She has come back).

Helen **has been in** Egypt for five years.(That's where she lives now).

## For/since:

For+period of time (for 5 days/months/years/weeks/minutes etc.)

**I haven't talked** to him **for** months.

Since+specific time (since yesterday/Monday/1990/last week etc.)

**I haven't talked** to him **since** last week.

Since + simple past       **but**       Present perfect + since

**I haven't talked** to Henry **since he moved** to New york.

It's year's/months/7 weeks/etc, since someone did something

**It's such a long time since I last saw** you.

It's(has) been year's/months/4 weeks/etc., since someone did something

**It's (has) been a long time since I last went** on vacation.

# Present perfect continuous
## Structure

I **have been lying** to you all these years.

I **have not been sleeping** well lately.

How long **have you been working out?**

We use present perfect continuous :

for an action that started at an **unspecified(indefinite)** time in the past and continues in the present.

I **have been working** on this book for three years

I **have been sleeping** for twelve hours.

for an action that **started in the** past but whose **results we can see in the present.** (We have evidence in the present time that something has been happening.)

**Your eyes are red.** Have you been crying?

**You look really exhausted.** Have you been working all night again.

**Expressions used with present perfect continuous:**
**For, since, all day/week/morning, lately, how long**

## PAST TENSES
### Past simple
**Structure:**
Most verbs in the past tense end in – **ed.** There is, however, a long list of irregular verbs at the end of the book that must be learned by heart.

Affirmative Sentences

| Subject | Verb(Past) |
|---|---|
| I | **worked** |
| You | **played** |
| He/she/it | **arrived** |
| We | **loved** |
| You | **ate(irregular)** |
| They | **saw(irregular)** |

Negative sentences

| Subject. | Auxiliary + Not | Infinitive | |
|---|---|---|---|
| I | **did not** | **listen** | to you. |
| You | **did not** | **work** | last night. |
| He/she/it | **did not** | **make** | noise. |
| We | **did not** | **eat** | ------- |
| You | **did not** | **swim** | ------- |
| They | **did not** | **drive** | to work. |

Interrogative Sentences

| Auxiliary | Subject | Verb(Infinitive) | |
|---|---|---|---|
| **Did** | **I** | **listen** | to you. |
| **Did** | **you** | **work** | last night. |
| **Did** | He/she/it | **make** | noise. |
| **Did** | **we** | **eat** | -------- |
| **Did** | **you** | **swim** | -------- |
| **Did** | **they** | **drive** | to work. |

We use simple past:

for an action that **happened and finished at a definite (specific) time in the past** even if the speaker doesn't mention the exact time. We are more interested in when the action happened, and not so much in what happened.

**I had a great time** at the party **last night.**

to express **past routines and habits.** It has the same meaning as "used to"

When I was in primary school **I woke up early** in the morning to watch cartoons.

for past actions happening one after the other.

When I was in school, **I woke up** early in the morning; **I took a shower, had breakfast, brushed my teeth** and **left for school**.

**Time expressions used with simple past:** a week ago, five days ago, last week/month/year, yesterday, the other day, on Monday, in 1980, in June, in the past, etc.

**Used to + bare infinitive ➲ past habits/facts/states**
**Used to** describes **past habits (actions)**, **facts** and **states** that are no longer true:

**Did John use to** drink when he was younger? ▸ habit.

**I used to like** school. ▸ state ( I don't like school any more.)

When I was little **I used to hate** spinach. ▸ state

**I used to believe** in God. ▸ state

**He used to be** smart. ▸ state

**I used to live** in America. ▸ fact

**I used to** be a vegetarian. ▸ state

**Would** (always, rarely, seldom, occasionally, constantly, often, never) + **bare infinitive➲ past habits /not facts or states**, and therefore is not used with stative verbs such as like, hate, enjoy, love, believe, remember etc. **With stative verbs we use "used to" instead:**

✓**I would/used to wake up** early in the morning when I was in school. (**past habit**)

x I ~~would like~~ school. (**state**)

✓I **used to like** school. (**state**)

**"Would"** has no interrogative form. We use **"used to"** instead:

✓**Did you use to wake up** early in the morning?

x Would you wake up early in the morning?

> "Would" in the negative changes the meaning of the sentence:

**When I was younger I would not smoke.**
(=I refused to Smoke.)

**but:**

**When I was younger I did not use to smoke.**
(=I didn't smoke then, but I do now.)

**Would always+bare infinitive:**

When I was a little girl **I would always** wake up early on Sunday morning to go to church.

### Past continuous (past progressive)

**Affirmative**

| subject | auxiliary verb (was/were) | main verb +ing | |
|---|---|---|---|
| I | was | listening | to music. |
| You | were | watching | TV. |
| He/she/it | was | annoying | me. |
| We | were | dancing | all night. |
| You | were | sleeping | ------------ |
| They | were | contemplating | ------------ |

**Negative**

| subject. | auxiliary verb | not | main verb+ing | |
|---|---|---|---|---|
| I | was | not | annoying | you. |
| You | were | not | working | last night. |
| He/she/it | was | not | making | noise. |
| We | were | not | disturbing | you. |
| You | were | not | enjoying | yourself. |
| They | were | not | lying | to you. |

## Interrogative

| auxiliary verb | subject | main verb+ing | |
|---|---|---|---|
| **Was** | I | dreaming? | |
| Were | you | pulling | my leg? |
| **Was** | he/she/it | sleeping? | ---------- |
| Were | we | imagining | it? |
| Were | you | putting | me on? |
| Were | they | pulling | my leg |

### Short forms: wasn't/weren't in the negative

I **wasn't** discussing politics with them.

He **wasn't** interested in the lecture.

You **weren't** informed about the cancellation of your flight.

### No short forms in the affirmative and interrogative

I was addressing an audience of five hundred people.

Was he interrupting us on purpose?

### Use
We use past continuous:

**to emphasize the duration of an action that took place at a particular or specific time in the past**

-What **were you doing** on Sunday morning?

-I **was sleeping** of course. What else would I be doing on Sunday Morning.

**to express a long action interrupted by a shorter one. We use simple past to refer to the short action**

I **was doing** the ironing when you **fell down** the stairs.

While I **was doing** the ironing, you **fell** down the stairs.

I **was sleeping** when the telephone **rang.**

What **were you doing** when I **came** home?

**to express two actions happening at the same time** in the past with "when" or "while"

I **was watching** TV **while** you **were talking** on the phone.

**to express frequently repeated actions in the past annoying to the speaker** with always, forever, constantly

She **was always telling** lies.

> Time expressions used with past continuous:
> **while, when, as**

**As/while** we were waking home, it started to rain.

**Stative verbs are not used in the past continuous:**

**Stative verbs:**
Action verbs express what a person does. **Stative verbs** express states continue over a period of time, rather than actions and **are not usually used in continuous tenses.** Here is a list of the most frequently used stative verbs:

| Senses | hear, see, smell, taste, feel, sound |
|---|---|
| Possession | have, own want, contain, belong to |
| Emotions | like, love, enjoy, hate, dislike, want, need, prefer, hope, wish, feel, forgive |
| Opinion | think, believe, suppose, agree, understand, seem |
| Measurement | weigh, cost, measure, equal |
| Mental states | know, remember, forget, mean, look(appear), mind |
| Other stative verbs | decide, resemble, tend, conclude, perceive, appreciate, recognize, be(exist), etc |

## Verbs used both in progressive and non- progressive tenses

When the following stative verbs are used in progressive tenses, they have a different meaning than when they are used in non-progressive tenses:

| Non-progressive | Progressive(continuous) |
|---|---|
| "**have**"with the meaning of possession | "**have**"enjoy one self |
| "**see**"look with the eyes | "**see**"meet or date someone |
| "**think**"believe | "**think**"someone's thoughts |
| "**feel**"describing someone's mood | "**feel**" touch |
| "**smell**" talking about how something smells | "**smell**"using one's nose to understand how something smells |
| "**be**"describing how you are | "**be**"behaving in a certain way |
| "**appear**"seem | "**appear**"give a performance, give a speech, etc |

## Past perfect
### Affirmative

| subject | had | past participle of the main verb | | |
|---|---|---|---|---|
| I | had | talked | to him | earlier. |
| You | had | seen | her | before the accident. |
| He/she/it | had | had | been there | before. |
| We | had | answered | the phone | when it went dead. |
| You | had | left | the house | when the burglary occurred. |
| They | had | finished | supper | before I came home. |

## Negative

| subject | had | not | past participle of the main verb | |
|---|---|---|---|---|
| I | had | not | talked | to her. |
| You | had | not | seen | her. |
| He/she/it | had | not | been | there. |
| We | had | not | answered | the phone. |
| You | had | not | left | the house. |
| They | had | not | finished | yet. |

## Interrogative

| had | subject | past participle of the main verb | |
|---|---|---|---|
| Had | I | talked | to her? |
| Had | you | seen | her? |
| Had | he/she/it | been | there? |
| Had | we | answered | the phone? |
| Had | you | left | the house? |
| Had | they | finished | finished? |

**Past perfect is used:**

for an action that happened and was completed in the past

Jane **had known** about it for a while.

in reported speech

John said to James, "Did you miss the bus?" ➔ John asked James if he **had missed** the bus.

to describe an action that happened in the past before another past action

I **had spent** all my money when I saw this really nice pair of shoes on sale.(=first I spent all my money and then I saw this really nice pair of shoes.)

I **had already left** the house when you came to see me.
(=first I left and then you came to see me.)

when using "before" or "after" in the sentence, although it's not always necessary to use past perfect because the meaning is clear

**After** you **had talked** to me, I went to bed.
(=first you talked to me and then I went to bed)
        or
**After** you **talked** to me, I went to bed.

after: "This was, it was, he was + SUPERLATIVE + Past perfect"

This was **the best** book (that) **I had ever read**.

It was **the most interesting** lecture **I had ever attended**.

After "It was /this was the first /second/last/only time+ Past Perfect"

**It was the first time** I had (that) ever said that.

> **Time expressions used with past perfect:**
> By the time, by, by then, already, when, after, before, never, just, for, since, yet

**By the time I got home, my roommate had already done** the house work.(=first my roommate did the house work, and then I went home.)

1$^{st}$ action ➲ my roommate did the housework.

2$^{nd}$ action ➲ I went home.

**By midnight, I had finished** studying.(=I finished studying before midnight.)

## Past perfect continuous

## Affirmative

| subject | had | been | verb + ing | | |
|---------|-----|------|------------|---|---|
| I | had | been | working | as a teacher | before I moved here. |
| You | had | been | living | in America | when I first saw you. |
| He/she/it | had | been | lying | to me | for years before I found out. |
| We | had | been | talking | on the phone | when the earthquake happened. |
| You | had | been | arguing | with him | when I entered the room. |
| They | had | been | discussing | business | at the time of the accident. |

Past perfect continuous is used:

to emphasize the continuity of an action before another past action

They won the dancing competition because **they had been practicing** really hard all year.

to express a past action which had visible results in the past

Her eyes were red because **she had been crying** all day.

> Time expressions used with past perfect continuous:
> **for, since, all day/ night/week/ month/year, how long**

When my great grand parents moved to America they had been married **for** nearly fifty years.

They didn't want to move to America because they hey had lived in Ireland **all their life.**

He was a wonderful pianist. He had been playing the piano **since** he was a teenager.

### Present perfect continuous vs past perfect continuous

Present Perfect Continuous for an action with **visible results in the present:**

I **am** late because **I have been working** all day.

Past Perfect Continuous for an action with **visible results in the past:**

I **was** late because **I had been working** all day.

## FUTURE TENSES
### *Future forms*
(Simple future(will)/going to/present continuous/simple present)

| | | |
|---|---|---|
| **Simple future(will)** | For a decision made at the moment of speaking: | It's too dark. I'll turn on the light.<br><br>It's cold. I'll close the window. |
| | For a promise: | I'll buy you some ice cream if you behave, children.<br><br>Don't worry mum, I'll drive carefully.<br><br>Trust me, I won't tell anyone what you told me. |
| | For a prediction after: **be afraid, believe, expect, think, hope, certainly, sure, perhaps, maybe, probably** | I'm afraid, he will be late for dinner.<br><br>He will probably get the job.<br><br>I believe, that this will be a good year for us. |
| | To express willingness to do something: | I'll help you find a dress for your prom.<br><br>You study for your exam, and I'll do your house work. |
| | To express refusal to do something: | I won't lie to your parents for you. |
| **Be going to:** | For an intention/plan: (used in informal style) | I'm going to do graduate studies. |

| **Present continuous:** | For a future plan: | I'm leaving for Hong Kong on Monday. I'm coming to see you soon. |
|---|---|---|
| **Simple present:** | For timetables: | The plane takes off at 7:00 pm tomorrow.<br><br>What time does the bus arrive in Boston.<br><br>My lesson starts at 5:00 pm tomorrow. The stores are open on the last Sunday before Christmas. |
| ** **Note:** "Will" is also used **to make a request.**<br>Will you help me set the table? |||

## More expressions used to talk about the future:

| be to: | For something that will happen or is scheduled to happen: | The meeting is to start in an hour. (=The meeting starts in an hour.) |
|---|---|---|
| **be due to/ be to:** | For something that is expected or planned to happen: | Our guests **are due/are to** arrive in the evening.<br><br>The meeting **is to/is due to** take place next week.<br><br>The baby **is due** in April.(...expected to be born)<br><br>**When is our composition due?** (=When is our composition to be handed in?) |

| | | |
|---|---|---|
| **be about to/ be on the point of:** | When something is ready to happen: | The meeting **is about to** begin.<br><br>She **was about to** go to sleep, when I arrived.<br><br>Helen **is on the point of** asking for a divorce. |
| **be on the verge of/be on the brink of+noun/ing** | When something is ready to happen: | I'm **on the verge of** a nervous breakdown.<br><br>I'm **on the verge of** tracing the culprit.<br><br>We are **on the brink of** war. |
| **be bound to/be likely to:** | For something that will probably happen or is certain to happen: | If you don't hurry up, **you're bound /likely to** be late for your appointment.<br><br>If you don't hurry up, **it is likely that** you'll be late for your appointment. |
| **be sure:** | When something is certain to happen: | **You are sure to** win. |
| **chances are:** | For something that will probably happen or not happen or is certain to happen or not happen: | **Chances are that** you will get the job. |

★**Be to is also used in conditionals to say what might happen:**

**If I were to** come with you on this trip, would you be pleased? (if I came with you ......)

**Were I** to come with you on this trip, would you be pleased? (⮕**Formal**)

### We do not use "Will" "Would" or "Going to after time and condition Conjunctions:

| | | |
|---|---|---|
| after | the moment | on condition that |
| as long as | the minute | as long as |
| as soon as | the next time | provided/providing that |
| immediately (=as soon as) | the sooner...the... | assuming that |
| before | once | only if |
| until | until/till | suppose/supposing that |
| by the time | (ever) since | |
| | when | even if/though |
| | whenever | if |
| | while | what if |
| | whilst (formal) (=while) | unless |
| | | in case |

We use the following to talk about something that **we meant to do in the future,** but for some reason it didn't happen:

**was going to, was about to, was to, was due to +bare infinitive**

I was going to call you, but I got caught up in traffic. (I didn't call you because I got caught up in traffic.)

**was on the verge of/ was on the brink of +ing or noun**

**I was on the verge/brink of** having a nervous breakdown when you called me and reassured me that you were okay.
( =If you hadn't called me, I might have had a nervous breakdown.)

## Future continuous

| Affirmative: | subject | + | will be | + | ing | | |
|---|---|---|---|---|---|---|---|
| Negative: | subject | + | will | + | not be | + | ing |
| Interrogative: | will | + | be | + | ing | | |

We use future continuous:

**to emphasize the duration of a future action**

Tomorrow at this hour **I will be lying** on the beach in Myconos.

When you wake up tomorrow morning, **I will still be flying** to Australia.

**to make polite requests** about somebody's intentions

**Will you be helping out** at the charity ball this weekend?

When **will we be seeing** you again?

## Future perfect

| Affirmative: | Subject | + | will have | + | past participle | | |
|---|---|---|---|---|---|---|---|
| Negative: | Subject | + | will not have | + | Past participle | | |
| Interrogative: | Will | + | subject | + | have | + | past participle |

We use future perfect **for an action that will be completed before another action in the future or before a specific time in the future:**

I **will have left** by the time you come home.

I **will have finished** all my Christmas shopping by tomorrow.

**Will you have cooked** dinner before the guests arrived?

> Time expressions used with future perfect:
> **by three, by tomorrow, by next year, by 2020, etc,
> by the time, before, until** ("until" can only be used
> in negative sentences)

The children **will have done** their homework **by** ten o'clock. ⮕correct

The children **will have done** their homework ~~until~~ ten o'clock. ⮕wrong ("until" can only be used in negative sentences")

The children **won't have done** their homework **by/until** nine o'clock. ⮕correct

### Future perfect continuous

| Subject | + | will have been | + | ing | | |
|---|---|---|---|---|---|---|
| Subject | + | will | + | not | + | have been | + | ing |
| Will | + | subject | + | have been | + | ing |

We use future perfect continuous to show that an action **will continue up until a specific time or event in the future** to emphasize the duration of an action:

By the time I retire, **I will have been working** for forty years.

When I leave work today, **I will have been talking** for over three hours.

> Time expressions used with future perfect continuous: by three, by tomorrow, by next year, by 2020, etc, by the time, before, until ("until" can only be used in negative sentences)

## QUESTION TAGS

Question tags **are small questions at the end of a sentence** used to ask **for confirmation to affirmative and negative sentences**. They are formed, **the same way we form questions**, with an **auxiliary verb + subject pronoun**:

**You are** English, **aren't you?**

Positive statement ⮕ negative question tag
Negative statement ⮕ positive question tag

You **are** sick, **aren't you?**

You **are not** sick, **are you?**

You **can** tell me, **can't you?**

**You don't like** me, **do you?**


If there is an auxiliary verb in the sentence, we use that auxiliary verb to form a question tag:

You **are** sick, **aren't you?**

He **will** come, **won't** he?

He **has left, hasn't he?**

If there is **no auxiliary verb in the sentence,** we use **do/does for simple present** and **did for simple past**:

You **work** hard, **don't you?**

You **don't work** hard, **do you?**

You **told** him, **didn't** you?

You **didn't tell** him, **did** you?

190

Everyone/everybody/someone/somebody/anyone/ anybody/no one/nobody/these/those take **"they" in the tag:**

**Everyone** came, didn't **they?**

**Someone** has told her, haven't **they?**

**Anybody** could have told him, couldn't **they?**

**Those are** mine, **aren't they?**

Everyone/everybody/somebody/someone/ anybody/ Anyone/ no one/nobody are used **with singular verbs:**

Everybody **believes** what you are saying, don't they?

Someone **is** absent, aren't they?

Nobody **likes** what you are doing, do they?

No one **is** home, are they?

**Nothing/this/that** take **"it"** in the tag:

**This is** absurd, **isn't it?**

**That's** finished, **isn't it?**

**Nothing was** done about it, **was it?**

**Hardly (ever), no(one), nothing, nobody, nowhere, neither, never, rarely, seldom, scarcely, barely,** are negative words which take an **affirmative tag:**

**Nobody** came, **did they?**

**Hardly** anyone came, **did they?**

**Never** forget this, **will you?**

**Nothing** was done about the matter, **was it?**

She can **barely** talk, **can she?**

The non-abbreviated question tag **not** is used at the end of a question tag. It is formal, however, and is very rarely used:

You will eventually tell me, **will you not?**
(=You will eventually tell me, **won't you?**)

You are the one who came up with the idea, **did you not?**
(=You are the one who came up with the idea, **didn't you?**)

**Isn't that true, don't you think, don't you know, don't you agree** are also used instead of a question tag:

You have finally decided not to drop out of school, **isn't that true?**

Steven proposed to Rachel, **isn't that true?**

She shouldn't trust him, **don't you agree?**

Smoking must not be permitted here, **don't you think?**

When we have **"there" in a sentence,** we can also use **"there" in the question tag:**

**There is** nothing to talk about, **is there?**

**There was** a misunderstanding, **wasn't there?**

**Positive statement ⇒ positive tag?** This is a special construction, used in tags, to express surprise:

He likes me, **he does?**

He told her, **he did?**

He's coming, **he is?**

## Special Question Tags:

| | | |
|---|---|---|
| 1) "I am" | "aren't I?" | I am late, **aren't I?** ⇨informal<br>I am late, **am I not**?⇨ formal |
| 2) "Let's" | "shall we?" | Let's begin, **shall we?** |
| 3) "Let me/her" etc | "will you?" | Let me help you, **will you/won't you?** |
| 4) Imperative (orders/requests) | "will /won't/ can/can't/ would you?" | Open the window, **will you/won't you/can you/can't you/would you?** ⇨imperative<br><br>Tell me, **will you/can you?** ⇨friendly request<br>Tell me, **won't you/can't you?** (This is a friendly request. The speaker is quite annoyed, though.) |
| 5) "Don't (negative imperative) | "will you?" | Don't leave, **will you?** ⇨negative imperative |
| 6) Polite suggestions/offers/ invitations | "won't you?" | Have a drink, **won't you?** ⇨polite offer<br>Consult a lawyer, **won't you?** ⇨polite suggestion |
| 7) "This is/That is" | "isn't it?" | This is final, isn't it? |
| 8) "I have" (possession) | "haven't I?" | He has three kids, **hasn't he?** ⇨possession |
| 9) "I have" (Idiom)<br>   "I had" | "don't I?"<br>"didn't I" | They had a nice time, **didn't they**⇨idiom |
| 10) "I used to" | "didn't I?" | They used to be friends, **didn't they?** |

| everybody/everyone/anybody |
|---|
| anybody/anyone |
| nobody/no one |
| neither |
| none |
| these/those |

⊃ become **"they"** in question tags

**Everybody is** sick today, **aren't they?**

**Nobody knows** what happened, **do they?**

**Those books are** mine, **aren't they?**

| everybody/everyone/anybody |
|---|
| anybody/anyone |
| nobody/no one |
| neither |
| none |
| these/those |

⊃ used with **singular verbs**

Everybody **knows** what you are saying. **don't they?**

Someone **is** absent. **aren't they?**

Nobody **knows** what you are doing. **do they?**

### Agreement to affirmative sentences
### So +auxiliary +subject
### or
### Subject +auxiliary +too

| | | |
|---|---|---|
| I like sports | **So does he** | **He does too** |
| He is studying | **So is she** | **She is too** |
| We missed the bus | **So did they** | **They did too** |
| I have finished | **So have we** | **We have too** |
| They had seen him | **So had we** | **We had too** |
| He will come | **So will they** | **They will too** |

## Agreement to negative sentences
### (Neither/nor +auxiliary +subject)
### or
### (Subject +auxiliary +not +either)

| I don't like football | **Neither/nor does she** | She doesn't either |
|---|---|---|
| He is not studying | **Neither/nor is she** | She isn't either |
| We didn't miss the bus | **Neither/nor did they** | They didn't either |
| I haven't finished yet | **Neither/nor have we** | We haven't either |
| They hadn't seen him | **Neither/nor had we** | We hadn't either |
| They won't see him | **Neither will we** | We won't either |

## Disagreement to affirmative sentences
### ( But +)subject pronoun/noun +negative auxiliary verb

| I like football | **He doesn't** | (I like football, **but he doesn't**) |
|---|---|---|
| John is studying | **Ann isn't** | (John is studying, **but Ann isn't**) |
| We missed the bus | **They didn't** | (We missed the bus, **but they didn't**) |
| I have finished | **We haven't** | (I have finished, **but we haven't**) |
| They had seen him | **We hadn't** | (They had seen him, **but we hadn't**) |
| He will come | **We will not** | (He will come, **but we will not**) |

## Disagreement to negative sentences

**( But +)subject pronoun/noun +affirmative auxiliary verb**

| I don't like football | **He does** | (I don't like football, **but he does**) |
|---|---|---|
| Tim is not studying | **Helen is** | (Tim is not studying, **but Helen is**) |
| We didn't miss the bus | **They did** | (We didn't miss the bus, **but they did**) |
| I haven't finished yet | **They have** | (I haven't finished yet, **but they have**) |
| They hadn't seen him | **We had** | (They hadn't seen him, **but we had**) |
| He will not come | **We will** | (He will not come, **but we will**) |

### So/not:

Using **so** and **not** in answers after the following verbs: **think, believe, expect, suppose, imagine, hope, seem, be afraid, appear, tell somebody.**

| Affirmative answers | Negative answers 1 | Negative answers 2 |
|---|---|---|
| I think so | I don't think so | I think not |
| I believe so | I don't believe so | I believe not |
| I expect so | I don't expect so | I expect not |
| I suppose so | I don't suppose so | I suppose not |
| I imagine so | I don't imagine so | I imagine not |
| It seems so | It doesn't seem so | It seems not |
| I'm afraid so | ----------------------- | I'm afraid not |
| I guess so | ----------------------- | I guess not |
| I hope so | ----------------------- | I hope not |

-Will you be coming to see us today?
**-I think so.** I have the day off.

-Is it going to be sunny this morning?
**-It seems so.** The sun is out already.

-Is Ann going to take part in the contest?
**-She told me so**. I hope she doesn't change her mind.

-Do you like our new neighbours?
**-I guess so**. They seem nice.

-Will you be moving to your new house soon?
**-I don't imagine so**. It still needs a lot of doing up.

## INDIRECT SPEECH (REPORTED SPEECH)

**Direct speech or quoted speech is giving a person's exact words using inverted commas (quotation marks ):**

She said, "I enjoy learning the correct usage of the language."

**Indirect speech is when we are reporting what someone has said:**

**She said** that she enjoyed learning the correct usage of the language.

### Introductory verbs most commonly used
**Tell someone something, say something, ask, replied.**
("Tell" is always followed by an object pronoun,( me,you,him, her, it, us, them,) or proper noun "Evans, Andrew," etc.)

**She told me** that she was coming the following week.
**I told Anthony** that I wasn't going to lie to his parents.
             but
**She said** that she was coming the following week.
**I said** that I wasn't going to lie to Anthony's parents.

## Punctuation

**Quotation marks or inverted commas(" ") are used to report somebody's exact words or thoughts:**

" I work hard,"

**A comma is placed after said if it's in the beginning:**

She said, "I work hard." " I work hard," she said.

**Quotation marks are added after the full stop:**

She said, "I work hard."


## Personal pronouns

Personal pronouns and possessive adjectives change, accordingly, when reporting someone else's words:

"**I** will not be able to see **you** tomorrow." She said.

She said that **she** would not be able to see **me** the following day.

## Tense changes

When we are reporting someone else's words the **tenses change if the introductory verb is in the simple past.** It is helpful to remember that we go one tense back into the past when we change the tenses in indirect speech:

"I **am** overjoyed" ➲She **said** that she **was** overjoyed.

"I **am** overjoyed" ➲She **says** that she **is** overjoyed.(no change)

198

| Direct speech | Indirect speech |
|---|---|
| She said, "I work hard."<br>"I work hard," she said. | She said (that) she worked hard. |
| She said, "I am working hard."<br>"I am working hard," she said. | She said (that) she was working hard. |
| She said, "I have worked hard."<br>"I have worked hard," she said. | She said (that) she had worked hard. |
| She said, "I have been working hard."<br>"I have been working hard," she said. | She said (that) she had been working hard. |
| She said, "I worked hard."<br>"I worked hard," she said. | She said (that) she had worked hard. |
| She said, "I was working hard."<br>"I was working hard," she said. | She said (that) she had been working hard. |
| She said, "I will work hard."<br>"I will work hard," she said. | She said (that) she would work hard. |
| She said, "I will be working hard."<br>"I will be working hard," she said. | She said (that) she would be working hard. |
| She said, "I can work hard."<br>"I can work hard," she said. | She said (that) she could work hard. |

| | |
|---|---|
| She said,"I may work hard."<br>"I may work hard," she said. | She said (that) **she might work** hard. |
| She said, "I must/have to work hard."<br>(obligation) | She said( that) **she had to work** hard. |
| She said, "I must be wrong"<br>(deduction, assumption)<br>"I must be wrong," she said. | She said (that) **she must be wrong.**(no change for deduction,assumption) |
| She said, "I am going to work hard."<br>"I am going to work hard," she said. | She said (that) **she was going to work** hard. |
| She said, "I needn't work hard."<br>"I needn't work hard," she said. | She said (that) **she didn't need to work** hard. |
| She said, "I didn't need to work hard."<br>"I didn't need to work hard," she said. | She said (that) **she hadn't needed to work** to work hard. |
| would, could, might, should, used to, ought to and had to, must (assumption, deduction) | **No change** |

**All the words of time and place change if the introductory verb is in the simple past:**

She said, "**I'm coming back** home **next year.**"

She said (that) **she was coming back** home **the following year.**

Changes of words of time and place:

| Direct speech | Indirect speech |
|---|---|
| today/ tonight/ this week/month/year | that day, that night, that week/month/year |
| yesterday | the day before/the previous day |
| last week/month/year | the week/month/year before/the previous week/month/year |
| a week/month/year ago | the week/month/year before/ the previous week/month/year |
| tomorrow | the day after/the next day/the following day |
| next week/month/year | the following week/month/year the next week/month/year |
| here | there |

"**I will be able** to give you an answer **next week**," he said.
**He said( that) he would be able** to give me an answer **the following week.**

" George **brought me** some good news **yesterday**," he said.
**He said,( that) George had brought him** some good news **the day before.**

**A number of other word changes:**

| Direct speech | Indirect speech |
|---|---|
| this | **that** |
| these | **those** |
| here | **there** |
| come | **go** |
| now | **then** |

He said, "**This is** the house I would like to buy."
He said **that was** the house he would like to buy.

She said, "**I want to come** with you to London."
She said **she wanted to go** with me to London.

**No changes are made in indirect speech if or when:**

the introductory verb is in simple present, present perfect or simple future

She says, "**I'm coming back** home next year."
She **says** (that) **she is coming back** home next year."

we are reporting a general truth

He said, "**The sun revolves** around the earth."
He said (that) **the sun revolves** around the earth.

we are reporting a permanent state

She said, "**I live** in London."
She said that **she lives** in London.

we have 2nd or 3rd conditional **even if** the introductory verb is in simple past

"If you had talked to me, I would have been able to help you." she said.
She said ( that )if I had talked to her, she would have been able to help me.

"If I were you, I would not miss this opportunity." She said.
She said that if she were me, she would not miss this opportunity.

we have unreal past

She said, "**It's time you answered** some questions."
She said (that) **it was time I answered** some questions.

She said, **"I would rather you had not come."**
She said (that) **she would rather we/ I had not come**.

The children said, "**We wish we didn't have** school today."
The children said (that) **they wished they didn't have school** today.

we have past perfect or past perfect continuous

He said, "**I had been working.**"
He said (that) **he had been working.**

we are reporting somebody's words right after they are said

The teacher told Irene, **"You are cheating on the test."**
The teacher told Irene that **she is cheating on the test.**

we have would, could, might, should, used to, ought to and had to, must (assumption, deduction) in the sentence

He said, "We should leave immediately"
He said (that) they should leave immediately.

He said, "I could try to help you."
He said, (that) she could try to help us.

He said, "Veronica **must be** sick."**(assumption)**
He said that Veronica **must be** sick.

but

"You **must inform** every one of the changes." He said. **(obligation)**
He said that **I had to inform** every one of the changes.

### Indirect Questions (reported questions)

**When reporting interrogative sentences** (questions) it is important to remember that **the sentences become affirmative:**

| Direct speech | Indirect speech |
|---|---|
| "What are you doing?" | **She asked me what I was doing.** |
| "Where are you going?" | **She asked me where I was going.** |
| "Why did you do that?" | **She asked me why I had done that.** |
| "What is your name?" | **She asked me what my name is/was.** |

Note: The following reported questions on the left are not correct because their structure **should be affirmative (subject + verb)** and not interrogative (auxiliary +subject):

| Wrong | Correct |
|---|---|
| ❌ She asked me what was I doing? | ✅ **She asked me what I was doing.** |
| ❌ She asked me where was I going? | ✅ **She asked me where I was going.** |
| ❌ She asked me why had I done that? | ✅ **She asked me why I had done that.** |
| ❌ She asked me what was my name? | ✅ **She asked me what my name is /was.** |

We use if/whether to report yes/no questions.
The word "whether" is usually more formal and is used when there is a choice between two things:

| Direct speech | Indirect speech |
|---|---|
| "Did you get enough rest?" | **He asked me if/whether I had gotten enough rest.** |

When we are reporting sentences with a time word such as **who, why, when, where, etc.**, we use the same time word:

| Direct speech | Indirect speech |
|---|---|
| "Where did you go last night?" | **He asked me where I had gone the previous night.** |
| "Why are you late?" | **He asked me why I was late.** |
| "When is she coming?" | **He asked me when she was coming.** |
| "Where do they live?" | **He asked me where they live.** |
| "Who has she been meeting?" | **He asked me who she had been meeting.** |

**Introductory verbs used when reporting interrogative sentences:** ask/want to know/wonder/inquire, etc.

## Reporting the imperative (orders, requests, suggestions)

### Positive Imperative ➲ tell/order/advise/ask etc+person+full infinitive

| Direct speech: | Indirect speech |
|---|---|
| "Leave the room." | He told me to leave the room. |

### Negative imperative ➲ tell/ order/advice/ask etc + person + (not) +full infinitive.

| Direct speech | Indirect speech |
|---|---|
| "Don't tell them" | He told me not to tell them. |
| "You should not leave ." | He advised me not to leave. |
| "Could you please not tell anybody." | He asked me not to tell anybody. |

### Verb+object or proper noun(sb) +full infinitive

| | | |
|---|---|---|
| advise | "You should consult a lawyer." | She advised me to consult a lawyer. |
| ask | "Could you please help me lift this box." | She asked Gus to help her lift that box. |
| allow | "You can go out and play." | She allowed us to go out and play. |
| beg | "Please keep this a secret." | She begged me to keep that a secret. |
| command | "Start training the cadettes." | He commanded us to start training the cadettes |
| forbid | "Kids, you are forbidden to go outside." | He forbade us to go outside. |
| invite | "Would you like to come to my party." | He invited me (to go )to his party. |
| instruct | "Make sure you read the label before you wash it." | He instructed her to first read the label before she washed it. |
| order | "Leave at this moment." | She ordered us to leave. |

| | | |
|---|---|---|
| permit | "You can smoke outside." | She permitted us to smoke outside. |
| remind | "Don't forget to set the alarm." | She reminded her to set the alarm. |
| Urge | "If you try hard you can achieve anything." | She urged me to try hard. |

**More introductory verbs:**

> Other introductory verbs used to report what someone said without using the exact words they said:

### Verb+ object pronoun/proper noun(sb) +full infinitive

| | | | |
|---|---|---|---|
| want | "I would like you to trust me." | He **wanted me to trust** him. | **Verb + full infinitive** |
| warn | "You'll catch a cold if you go outside without your coat on." | She **warned me not to go** outside without my coat on. | |

| | | |
|---|---|---|
| agree | "Yes, I'll come with you." | She **agreed to come** with me. |
| decide | "I'll stay home and relax today." | She **decided to stay** home and relax that day. |
| demand | "I have to see you immediately." | He **demanded to see** me immediately. |
| offer | "I'll help you clean up." | He **offered to help** me clean up. |
| promise | "I'll take you to the cinema tomorrow." | He **promised to take** me to the **cinema the following day.** |
| prefer | "I would rather stay home." | He **prefers to stay** home. |

| refuse | "No, I won't help you." | He **refused to help** me. |
|---|---|---|
| threaten | "I will punish you if you go out, kids" | He **threatened to punish** us if we went out. |
| volunteer | "I'll babysit tonight, so you can go out." | She **volunteered/offered to babysit** that night so that we could go out.. |

## verb+ that clause

| admit | "**I stole** your USB." | He **admitted that he had stolen** my USB. |
|---|---|---|
| agree | "Why not, **I'll come** with you." | He **agreed that he would come** with me. |
| announce | "We're getting married the 15th of August." | They announced that they were getting married the 15th of August. |
| boast | "No one is more experienced than me." | He boasted that no one was more experienced than him. |
| claim | "I am a descendant of Alexander the Great. | He claimed that he was a descendant of Alexander the Great. |
| complain | "You always go to work late." | He complained that I always went to work late." |
| comment | "What a touching story!" | He commented that it was a touching story.<br>or<br>He commented on how touching the story was. |
| decide | "I made up my mind. I'm going to Spain on my vacation." | He decided that he was going to Spain on his vacation. |
| deny | "I never cheated in an exam." | He denied that he had ever cheated in an exam. |

| | | |
|---|---|---|
| exclaim | "You won!" "What a beautiful day!" | He exclaimed that I had won. He exclaimed that it was a beautiful day. or He exclaimed what a beautiful day it was. |
| explain | "You have to beat the eggs before putting them in the pan." | He explained that I had to beat the eggs before putting them in the pan. |
| insist | "He should be informed immediately." | I insist that he be informed immediately.(subjunctive). |
| recommend | "You should definitely try that new Chinese restaurant." | He recommended that I try that new Chinese restaurant.(subjunctive) |
| report | "Several people have been arrested." | It was reported that several people had been arrested. |
| propose | "We should not act in haste." | I propose that we not act in haste.(subjunctive) |
| suggest | "You should be more alert." | He suggested that I be more alert.(subjunctive) |
| threaten | "If you don't cooperate" I will have to dismiss you." | He threatened that he would dismiss me if I didn't cooperate. |
| reassure | "Don't worry about the kids .I'll look after them." | He reassured me that he would look after the kids. |

## verb+gerund

| | | |
|---|---|---|
| admit | "I stole your USB." | He **admitted stealing** my USB. |
| deny | "I never cheated in an exam." | He **denied** ever **cheating** in an exam. |
| recommend | "We should try that new Chinese restaurant." | He **recommends trying** that new Chinese restaurant. |
| | "We should have breakfast before we go to work." | I **recommend having** breakfast before going to work. |
| suggest | "Do you feel like going dancing?" | He **suggested going** dancing. |
| | "How about watching some TV?" | He **suggested watching** some TV. |
| | "Let's play cards." | He **suggested playing** cards. |

## verb+preposition+gerund

| | | |
|---|---|---|
| apologise for | "I'm sorry for offending you." | He **apologised** for **offending** me. |
| boast about | "I'm the smartest." | He **boasted** about **being** the smartest. |
| insist on | 'They still play their music after midnight despite the complaints." | They **insist** on **playing** their music after midnight. |
| complain about | "I'm always working late." | He**'s always complaining about working** late. |

## Verb+ object(sb)+preposition+gerund

| | | |
|---|---|---|
| accuse someone of | "He lied to me." | **She accused** him **of lying** to her. |
| blame someone for | "I ran over a cat because of you." | **He blamed me for running** over a cat. |
| congratulate someone on | "Congratulations! You passed the proficiency exam." | **He congratulated me on passing** the proficiency exam. |
| complain to somebody about | "I'm always working late." | **He's always complaining to me about working** late. |

The subjunctive is used in reported speech with some verbs when there is a change of subject, or when we have a "that clause". It is used regardless of time reference to talk about present, past and future.

**Introductory verb+ that clause+ bare infinitive**
**or**
**Introductory Verb+ that clause+ should +bare infinitive**

**Verbs:**
advise/ agree/ ask/ beg/ hope/(would)prefer/petition/ suggest/recommend/propose/ request/ require/ demand/command/order/ insist /urge /desire/ whisper/vote etc:

     Direct speech
**I said, "He should see a doctor."**

     Indirect speech
**I suggest he see a doctor.**
**I suggest that he should see a doctor.**

With some verbs when there is no change of subject the gerund can be used:

     Direct speech                          Indirect speech
**He said, "Let's go home." He suggested going home . ⮑gerund**

## MODAL VERBS

Modal verbs are special **verbs that give extra information about the main verb** that comes after the modal verb:

You **must tell** me the truth.

You **should see** a doctor.

You **should sleep** more.

**All modal verbs** except the verb "ought to" are **followed by bare infinitive:**

You **should** study.

She **must** be sick.

You **ought to** tell me the truth.

You **ought to** see a doctor.

You o**ught to** sleep more.

**Modal verbs do not take "s"** in the third person singular:

He **must** tell me the truth.

She **should** see a doctor.

He **should** sleep more.

He **can** speak three languages.

**Questions** are formed **by inverting modal verb and subject:**

**Should she** see adoctor?

**Should he** sleep more?

**Can he** speak more languages?

**Negations** are formed **by inserting "not" after the modal verb:**

He **must not** tell me the truth.

She **should not** see a doctor.

He **should not** sleep more.

He **can not** speak three languages.

**Modal verbs** and **auxiliary verbs** are used to **form short answers:**

Yes, **you should.**

No, **you can't.**

Yes, **we must.**

No, **you needn't.**

No, **I won't.**

Yes, **I do.**

Yes, **I am.**

When we use modal verbs, present, past, and future are **expressed** with **their corresponding infinitives:**

| | |
|---|---|
| **Present infinitive** <br> He must tell the truth | **do** |
| **Present continuous infinitive** <br> He must be telling the truth. | **be doing** |
| **Perfect infinitive** <br> He must have told the truth. | **have done** |
| **Perfect continuous infinitive** <br> He must have been telling the truth. | **have been doing** |

| | | |
|---|---|---|
| **may/might** | request permission, perhaps | **May I use** your pen?<br><br>John **may get mad** if you don't tell him the truth. |
| | **might/may as well** (=no other alternative) | There's a snow storm, so **we might as well stay home** and watch a movie on TV. |
| **must** | affirmative deduction, assumption | You **must** be sick. You look pale. |
| | affirmative obligation, necessity | You **must** see a doctor immediately! |
| **musn't** | negative obligation, necessity | You **mustn't** eat junk food. |
| **should** | advice in "that" clauses (subjunctive), (with verbs like **suggest, recommend, propose, insist, require request etc.** | **I suggest** that he (should) **sleep** more.<br><br>Some doctors **recommend** that their patients (should) stop smoking a few weeks before surgery. |

| | | |
|---|---|---|
| | **advice in "that" clauses (subjunctive) with adjectives like it is important/essential/ necessary/urgent/ vital)** | It is important that he (should) follow the instructions. |
| | | It is urgent that you (should) take the next flight home. |
| | | It is necessary that soldiers (should) always follow the orders of their superiors. |
| **ought to** | advice | **You ought to call** your parents. |
| **will** | future reference | **I will talk to him** as soon as I can. **They will probably be late** again. |
| | future prediction | **There will be rain tonight** in the north of the country. **They will probably be late** again. |
| | decision made on the spot | It's hot in here. **I'll turn on the air conditioning.** |

| | | |
|---|---|---|
| shall | future reference **although used on rare occasions** | **I shall not be able to come.** |
| | asking for advice although used rarely. | Where shall we go for dinner? |
| | "Should "is used more often rather than "shall"in question tags (small questions at the end of a sentence used to ask for confirmation to affirmative and negative sentences.) | Lets go to the movies, **shall we?** |
| can | ability in the present or future | **I can help** you with the house work, if you'd like. |
| | permission | You **can go**. Class is dismissed. |
| could | polite requests | **Could I have** a glass of water, please? |
| | ability in the past | When he was 5 **he could speak** three languages. |
| can't/couldn't | lack of ability | **I couldn't fix** the leaky faucet so I called the plumber. |
| | negative deduction, assumption | He **can't be** thirty. He looks over fifty. |

"**Can" and "could"** have no infinitive form and **no tenses other than present with "can" and past with "could."** We use **"be able to"** when we want to use other tenses.

| I (can) am able to | I (could) was able to | I have been able to | I will be able to | I will have been able to |
|---|---|---|---|---|

## "needn't" vs "didn't need to"

| need to | necessity | **You need to hurry.** |
|---|---|---|
| **needn't** | lack of necessity (you did something although it wasn't necessary) | John and Mary called to say they were not coming. **I needn't have cooked dinner.** (=I had already cooked dinner before I found out that they were not coming.) |
| **didn't need to** | lack of necessity (it wasn't necessary and you didn't do it) | John and Mary called to say they were not coming. **I didn't need to cook dinner.** (=I found out that they were not coming, so I didn't cook dinner.) |

| | "would" | |
|---|---|---|
| **would** | used in 2$^{nd}$ and 3$^{rd}$ conditionals | If he were more qualified, **he would be** eligible for the job.<br><br>If he had gone to college, **he would have had** better job prospects. |
| | used as the past form of **"will"** in reported speech | You promised you **would not be** late. |
| **would** | used to express repetition in the past | **When I was a kid,** I would wake up **very early on Sunday morning to watch cartoons.** |
| | polite requests | **Would you help** me lift this box, please? |

Although the following verbs behave like modal verbs, they are not modal verbs:

| | | |
|---|---|---|
| **have to** | necessity obligation but not as strong as "must" | **You have to go** to school. |
| | certainty | That **has to be** Steve. They said he's tall and blond. |
| **have got to** | necessity, obligation but not as strong as "must" | **I have got to finish** writing this grammar book by Christmas. |
| | certainty | The robbers **have got to have known** where the money was hidden. |
| **had better** | strong advice, threats | It's getting late. **You'd better go** now before it gets dark.<br><br>**You'd better start** studying harder or you'll flunk your test tomorrow. |

**Be to**=for something that will happen or is scheduled to happen

All **the students are to pass** an oral exam at the end of the course.

## Modal infinitives

When we use modal verbs Present, past, and future are expressed with their **corresponding infinitives:**

| Present infinitive **He must tell the truth** | **do** |
|---|---|
| Present continuous infinitive **He must be telling the truth.** | **be doing** |
| Perfect infinitive **He must have told the truth.** | **have done** |
| Perfect continuous infinitive **He must have been telling the truth.** | **have been doing** |

## Tenses corresponding with the infinitives

**{Present infinitive/present continuous infinitive/perfect infinitive/ perfect continuous infinitive}**

| Simple present | Present infinitive |
|---|---|
| He **is** probably at work. | He **must be** at work. (positive deduction). |
| He **is** probably not at work. | He **can't be** at work.(negative deduction) |
| **Simple future** | |
| He **will have to** work. | He **must work.** ( affirmative obligation) |
| He **will not have to** work. | He **must not work.** (negative obligation) |
| **Present/future continuous** | **Present continuous infinitive** |
| Maybe **he's working** | He **might be working.** |
| Maybe **he will be working.** | |
| **Simple past/present perfect/ past perfect** | **Perfect infinitive** |
| Maybe he **worked.** | He **might have worked.** |
| Maybe he **has worked.** | |
| Maybe he **had worked.** | |
| **Past continuous /present perfect continuous /past perfect continuous** | **Perfect continuous infinitive** |
| He **was probably working.** | He **must have been working.** |
| He **has probably been working.** | |
| He **had probably been working.** | |

## Helping verbs or auxiliary verbs

The following verbs can be used both as helping verbs(auxiliary verbs) and as main verbs:

### do, be, have, will, shall

When used as helping verbs, they are always followed by a main verb:

Do you **speak** English?

I am **reading** the paper at the moment.

Have you **finished** studying?

Will you be **coming** to see us this weekend?

When used as helping verbs, **"do" "does"** are used to form the **interrogative**, and **"don't" "doesn't"** to form the **negative** in the simple present. **"Did"** is used to form the **interrogative** and **"didn"** is used to form the **negative in the simple past:**

**Do you speak** English?

I **don't** like horror films.

**Did you read** your mail?

**I didn't go** to work today.

**"Am" "is" "are"** are used with the present participle to form present continuous, **"be"** is used with the present participle after modal verbs to form continuous types (present continuous, past, future continuous, and future perfect continuous, and with the past participle to form passive voice. **"Was," " were"** are used with the present participle to form past continuous:

I **am not going** to work today.

He **must be** sleeping.

I **will not be visiting** my parents this Christmas.

I **was hoping** you would call.

"Have" is used with the past participle to form perfect tenses (present perfect, present perfect continuous, past perfect, past perfect continuous, future perfect and future perfect continuous):

**Have you seen** any good films lately?

The kids **have ben lying** lately.

The house **has been broken** into.

**"Will"** is used with a bare infinitive to form future tenses:

**Will you be coming** to see me this week end?

## ADJECTIVES/ADVERBS

**Use:**
**An adjective describes or modifies a noun or a pronoun** or comes after certain verbs, **be, feel, look, seem, sound, smell, taste etc.** to describe how something is:

He is a **fast** driver.
He is a **careful** driver.
He **looks tired.**
I **feel sick.**
I feel **optimistic** about the outcome of the elections.
The stew tastes **delicious.**

Adjectives used to talk about **how somebody feels** end in **-ed:** **bored, interested, disappointed, excited, surprised:**

I am interested **in reading science fiction books.**

I'm so bored **today.**

Adjectives used to talk about how **something has influenced somebody** end in **-ing:** **boring, interesting, disappointing, exciting, surprising:**

**I find science fiction books** interesting.

**What a** boring **day this is**!

Adjectives have no plural form and no gender:

| a **beautiful** girl | **beautiful** girls |
| a **good-looking** man | **good-looking** men |

Nouns can also be used as adjectives. **When nouns are used as adjectives they are always singular:**

| ☑ **cat food** | ☒ **cats food** |
|---|---|
| ☑ **apple juice** | ☒ **apples** juice |
| ☑ **a five-day trip** | ☒ a five-**days** trip |
| ☑ **a ten-year-old boy** | ☒ a ten-**years**-old boy |
| ☑ **a four-week vacation** | ☒ a four-**weeks** vacation |

It is not unusual in English to use more than one adjective before a noun. **The correct order of adjectives in a sentence is the following:**

**Opinion +size+ age+ shape + color+origin(nationality)+ material +purpose +noun**

A bright tall thirty–year old thin Greek woman

A big one-family country house

**Structure:**

Adjectives that end in **-e** form their adverbs by adding **-ly** to the ending.

| **Adjective** | **Adverb** |
|---|---|
| rare | rarely |

Adjectives that end in **-le** preceded by a consonant form their adverbs by **dropping the -le and adding -ly.**

| **Adjective** | **Adverb** |
|---|---|
| simple | simply |
| favorable | favorably |

Adjectives that end in **-le** preceded by a vowel form their adverbs by **just adding-ly to the adjective.**

| Adjective | Adverb |
|-----------|--------|
| sole | solely |

EXCEPTION: In the case of **"whole"** the final **-e** is removed before adding the **-ly.**

**whole**                                              **wholly**

Adverbs answer the questions, **where? when? how? why?** and **to what extent?** An adverb describes or modifies a verb, an adjective or another adverb :

**He** drives fast.

**He** drives very carefully.

**He** waited patiently **for the results to come out.**

**The** well-recited poem **left everyone speechless.**

**Everyone was at a loss for words at the** wonderfully-performed play.

Unfortunately, **we did not arrive in time for the Christmas feast yesterday.**

Some words that end in **-ly** are used both as adjectives and adverbs: **daily, weekly, yearly, monthly, lonely, ugly, awful, friendly:**

**We have** weekly teachers' meetings. **(adjective)**

**We** meet weekly **to talk about our students.(adverb)**

**She's an** awful person. **(adjective)**

**She** talks awful.**(adverb)**

Adjectives that **end in –ly** should not be confused with adverbs:

Maria has **weekly** sessions with her shrink. (adjective)

Maria sees her shrink **weekly.**(adverb)

**Some irregular adverbs have the same adjective form:**

| Adjective | Adverb |
|---|---|
| fast | fast |
| hard | hard |
| early | early |
| awful | awful |
| late | late |
| high | high |
| low | low |
| near | near |
| deep | deep |
| wide | wide |
| lovely | lovely |

| Adjective | Adverb |
|---|---|
| He is an **awful person**. | The kids are behaving **awful** today. |
| He is a **fast driver**. | He drives **fast**. |
| He has **high grades**. | He climbed **high**. |
| She has **low grades**. | He stooped really **low**. |
| He's a **hard worker**. | He works **hard**. |
| I'm **near-sighted**. | I live **near** the subway. |

We distinguish adjectives from adverbs that have the same form by identifying what they describe.
**An adjective describes a noun** where **as an adverb describes a verb:**

I had a bad **day.**(adjective)

I **work** hard.(adverb)

When **fast, hard, early, late, low, high, awful, wide, deep, near** take the suffix –**ly** to form their adverbs, their meaning is different than that of their adjectives:

| | |
|---|---|
| **Deeply (extremely)** | I'm **deeply** touched. |
| **Hardly (almost never)** | I **hardly** ever see you any more. |
| **Widely (to a large extent)** | A controversial topic is something **widely** discussed. |
| **Lately (recently)** | Have you seen any good films **lately**? |
| **Nearly (almost)** | We've been living here for **nearly** ten years. |
| **Awfully (very)** | I am **awfully** tired. |
| **Highly (very)** | It is **highly** unlikely that he'll show up for dinner. He's **highly regarded/esteemed** for his ethics. (respected) |

We use **"bad" with state verbs** and **"badly" with action verbs**. However some **verbs that describe feelings can be both action verbs and state verbs.** You have to know the meaning that the specific verb wants to convey.

We use the adjective **"bad" to describe emotions, feelings and states** and the adverb **"badly" to descrive actions**:

I feel **bad**
You are **bad**
The kids are behaving **badly**
The dog smells **badly** (=he doesn't have the ability to smell using his nose)
The dog smells **bad** (=he needs a bath)
I need to see you **badly** (=very much)

## THE COMPARATIVE AND SUPERLATIVE OF ADJECTIVES

We use the comparative to compare two people or things and the superlative to compare two or more people or things.

To form the comparative and the superlative of **one-syllable adjectives** ( short adjectives) **with more than one vowel or more than one consonant** at the end of the word we use **-er** for the comparative and **-est** for the superlative:

| Adjective | Comparative | Superlative |
|---|---|---|
| old | older | oldest |
| fast | faster | fastest |
| new | newer | newest |
| short | shorter | shortest |
| smart | smarter | smartest |

You're **much older than I thought** you were.

She's **the oldest athlete in the team.**

For one syllable adjectives ending in **-e** we add **-r** to the adjective to form the comparative and **-est** to form the superlative:

| Adjective | Comparative | Superlative |
|---|---|---|
| nice | nicer | nicest |

For one syllable adjectives with 1 vowel and 1 consonant at the end of the word we double the consonant and add **-er** to form the comparative and -est to form the superlative:

| Adjective | Comparative | Superlative |
|---|---|---|
| big | bigger | biggest |
| fat | fatter | fattest |
| sad | sadder | saddest |
| hot | hotter | hottest |

For two-syllable adjectives ending in -y we change the -y to an -i and add -er to the adjective to form the comparative and -est to form the superlative:

| Adjective | Comparative | Superlative |
|-----------|-------------|-------------|
| sunny | sunnier | sunniest |
| happy | happier | happiest |
| pretty | prettier | prettiest |
| stuffy | stuffier | stuffiest |
| stingy | stingier | stingiest |

For two or more syllable adjectives (longer adjectives) that do not end in -y we add -more or -less before the adjective to form the comparative and -the most or -the least for the superlative:

| Adjective | Comparative | Superlative |
|-----------|-------------|-------------|
| beautiful | more beautiful | the most beautiful |
| interesting | more interesting | the most interesting |
| bored | more bored | the most bored |
| boring | more boring | the most boring |
| excited | more excited | most excited |

For some two or more syllable adjectives (longer adjectives) that do not end in -y we add -er before the adjective to form the comparative and -est for the superlative:

| Adjective | Comparative | Superlative |
|-----------|-------------|-------------|
| clever | cleverer | cleverest |
| quick | quicker | quickest |

Adjectives that are hyphenated (compound adjectives) form their comparative with **-more** and superlative with **—the most:**

Nick is **more hard-working than** John.

Nick is **the most hard-working boy** in the class.

**Adjectives that have irregular comparative and superlative forms:**

| Adjective | Comparative | Superlative |
|---|---|---|
| **good** | better | best |
| **bad** | worse | worst |
| **far** | farther | farthest |
| **far** | further | furthest |
| **little** | less | least |
| **much** | more | most |
| **many** | more | most |

This is **the best performance I have ever seen.**

You're **better at Maths than me.**

People nowadays have **less money than they used to** 20 years ago.

He is the least likely to win the contest.

Expressions used in the superlative: **in the world, of them all, I have ever seen/been to,** etc:

Vatican City is the **smallest country in the world.**

Los Angeles is one of the **nicest places I have ever been to.**

Two-Syllable Adjectives that can be used both with **-er** and **-est** and with **-more** and **–the most:**

| Two-Syllable Adjective | Comparative Form | Superlative Form |
|---|---|---|
| **clever** | cleverer/ more clever | cleverest /most clever |
| **friendly** | friendlier/ more friendly | friendliest/ most friendly |
| **funny** | funnier/ more funny | funniest/ most funny |
| **gentle** | gentler /more gentle | gentlest/ most gentle |
| **quiet** | quieter/ more quiet | quietest/ most quiet |
| **simple** | simpler /more simple | simplest /most simple |

The kids in my English class are **friendlier than /more friendly than** the kids in my Math class.

The kids in my English class are **the friendliest/ the most friendly** in the whole school.

## THE COMPARATIVE AND SUPERLATIVE OF ADVERBS

Adverbs answer the questions, **where? when? how? Why?** and **to "what extent?"**
An adverb describes or modifies a verb, an adjective or another adverb :

He **drives fast.**
He drives very **carefully.**
He waited **patiently** for the results to come out.
The **well-recited** poem left everyone speechless.
Everyone was at a loss for words at the **wonderfully-performed** play.
**Unfortunately,** we did not arrive in time for the Christmas feast yesterday.

One syllable adverbs **take -er to form the comparative and -est to form the superlative:**

| Adverb | Comparative | Superlative |
|--------|-------------|-------------|
| hard | harder | hardest |
| fast | faster | fastest? |

One or two syllable adverbs **ending in -ly become -lier to form the comparative and -liest to form the superlative:**

| Adverb | Comparative | Superlative |
|--------|-------------|-------------|
| **lovely** | lovelier | loveliest |
| **early** | earlier | earliest |
| **quickly** | quicklier | quickliest |

**For adverbs formed by adding the suffix -ly to the adjectives we form the comparative with –more or -less and the superlative with -most or -least:**

| Adjective | Adverb | Comparative Adverb | Superlative Adverb |
|---|---|---|---|
| **slow** | slowly | more slowly | most slowly |
| **happy** | happily | more happily | most happily |
| **quiet** | quietly | more quietly | most quietly |
| **careful** | carefully | more carefully | most carefully |

**For two or more syllable adverbs we use -more or -less before the adverb to form the comparative and -most or -least to form the superlative:**

| Adjective | Adverb | Comparative Adverb | Superlative Adverb |
|---|---|---|---|
| **interesting** | interestingly | more interestingly | most interestingly |
| **beautiful** | beautifully | more beautifully | most beautifully |
| **diligent** | diligently | more diligently | most diligently |

## Irregular adverbs:

**Some irregular adverbs that have the same adjective form take the suffix -er to form the comparative and -est to form the superlative:**

| Adjective | Adverb | Comparative Adverb | Superlative Adverb |
|---|---|---|---|
| **fast** | fast | faster | fastest |
| **hard** | hard | harder | hardest |
| **early** | early | earlier | earliest |
| **late** | late | later | latest |
| **high** | high | higher | highest |
| **low** | low | lower | lowest |
| **near** | near | nearer | nearest |
| **deep** | deep | deeper | deepest |
| **wide** | wide | wider | widest |
| **lovely** | lovely | lovelier | loveliest |

The following adverbs, **hardly, nearly, lately, deeply, widely,** have a different meaning than their adjectives:

| Nearly= | **almost** |
|---|---|
| Hardly= | **very rarely, very little** |
| Lately= | **recently** |
| Deeply= | **very** |
| Widely= | **by a lot of people** |

I **hardly** know him(=I know him very little.)

I'm so busy with work and all that I **hardly** go out any more.(=I very rarely go out.)

I haven't seen him **lately.** I don't know what he's up to.(=I haven't seen him recently.)

I **nearly** fell and broke my leg.(=I almost fell and broke my leg.)

## More comparisons:

**(Just, nearly)As +adjective/adverb + as** ➲ **in affirmative and interrogative sentences**

Mary Ann works **(just)** **as diligently as** her sister.

Mary Ann is **(just) as diligent as** her sister.

**Not as/so/+ adjective/adverb+ as** ➲ **in negative sentences**

Anthony doesn't work **as/so/ hard as** Jim.

**Not quite/nearly as +adjective/adverb+as**

Anthony doesn't work **quite/nearly as hard as** Jim.

**As much +uncountable noun + as**

Does Sofia have **as much free time as** her youngest sister?

**As many +countable plural noun +as**

I don't have **as many friends as** I used to.

**The + comparative..., the +comparative**

**The harder** you study, **the better** you do.

**Comparative + and + comparative**

People work **harder and harder** everyday to make ends meet.

236

### By far the + superlative

She is **by far** the best student.

### Much(far) + comparative adjective

You're **much smarter** than you think.

You're **far better** than me.

### Many more + plural countable noun

I've been to **many more** places than you have.

### Much more (+uncountable noun)

I know **much more** than you do.

I have **much more** experience in this job than you.

### Far too+adjective

He's **far too smart** to turn down this job offer.

## Fewer vs less

### We use fewer to compare countable plural nouns

I have **fewer questions** than I did when I first started this course.

### We use less to compare uncountable nouns

Nowadays, kids have **less free time** than they did in the past.

I have **less money** now than I did when I was working two jobs.

### Also: **most=very**

I was **most touched** by your kind gesture. (=I was very touched by your kind gesture.)

## THE DEFINITE ARTICLE (THE)

**The Definite Article is used with both singular and plural countable and uncountable nouns**:

| | |
|---|---|
| • to refer to something specific ☞ | • **The girls** are playing in the yard. |
| • to refer to a group (type of animal, musical instrument, machine, etc.) ☞ | • **The tiger** is becoming extinct.<br>• He plays both **the piano** and **the guitar.**<br>• **The typewriter** has become obsolete. |
| • with various adjectives used as nouns (the young, the elderly, the poor, the rich, etc.) ☞ | • The elderly need affection.<br>• The poor should be provided for by the state. |
| • before titles (the King, the President, etc.) ☞ | • **The headmaster** reprimanded the students.<br>• **The president** of the company has resigned. |
| • before the names of newspapers (The London Times, the New York Times, The International Herald Tribune, etc.) ☞<br>**Exceptions:** foreign newspapers: Le Figaro, Athens News, etc. | •**The New York Times** is an American daily newspaper.<br><br>• **The international Herald Tribune** is the Global edition of the New York Times. |
| • before surnames to refer to all the members of the family(the Smiths,the Bushes, the Jacksons, etc.) ☞ | • **The Johnsons** moved house. |

Helen Boubouli — Grammar Genie

| | |
|---|---|
| • **to talk about nationalities when referring to groups of people** (the Spanish, the British, etc.) ☞ | • **The British are fairly punctual.** |
| •**to talk about languages** (the Greek language, the French language etc.) | • **The English language** is widely spoken.<br>also<br>(=**English** is widely spoken.)<br><br>• **The French language** used to be more popular.<br>also<br>(= **French** used to be more popular.) |
| • **before rivers** (The Thames, The Mississippi, The Volga.) ☞ | • **The Volga** is the largest river in Europe. |
| • **before mountain ranges** (The Himalayas, The Alps, The Pyrenees, etc.) ☞ | **The Alps** are the highest mountain range system in Europe. |
| • **before seas or oceans** (the Mediterranean Sea, the Pacific Ocean, the Caribbean Sea, etc.) ☞ | • **The Atlantic Ocean** is the second-largest of the world's oceanic divisions. |
| • **before groups of islands** (the Virgin Islands, the Canary islands etc.) ☞ | • **The US Virgin Islands** is a vacation paradise. |
| • **with the superlative** (the best, the smartest, the most, the worst, etc.) ☞ | • This is **the most delicious meal** I have ever had. |
| • **before objects that are regarded as unique** (the Eiffel Tower, The Parthenon, The Colosseum, the Tower of Pisa, the Sun, the Moon, the Stars, the Sea, the Earth, etc.) | •The Parthenon is the most important surviving building of Classical Greece. |
| **Exceptions**: **Big Ben** | **Big Ben is** the nick name for the Great Bell of the clock in London. |

## The definite article is omitted:

| | |
|---|---|
| • when we are not talking about something specific. ☞ | • I bought a house. |
| • to refer to something in general with uncountable or plural nouns. ☞ | • **English** is an international language.<br>also<br>(=The English language………)<br><br>• **Physics** is my favourite subject in school.<br><br>• **Teenagers** are known to rebel. |
| • before abstract nouns (love, beauty, peace, etc.) ☞ | **Peace** is when people are able to resolve their conflicts without violence.<br><br>**Beauty** is in the eye of the beholder. |
| • before lakes( Lake Michigan, Lake Wanapitei, etc.)☞ | •**Lake Michigan** is the largest lake in the United States. |
| • before continents(Asia, Africa, Europe, etc.) ☞ | •**Europe** is one of the worlds seven continents. |
| • before countries or cities (Greece, France, Italy, Paris, Athens, New york,etc.)☞ | •Athens is the capital and largest city of Greece. |
| • before names (James Brown, Mr Smith, etc.)☞ | **Rowan Atkinson** is the name of the guy who played **Mr Bean**. |

- **before certain words when we are referring to their use and not to the buildings or to the structure** (home, hospital, church, town, work, university, college, bed, prison, high school, junior high, primary school.) ☞

• It's time for the kids to **go to bed.**
(=It's time for the kids to go to sleep.)
       but
• Please don't leave your clothes on the bed.
(= We are talking about the bed itself.)

• My eldest **goes to college.**
(=He is a college student.)
       but
• The college that I go to was built in 1920.)
(=Here we're talking about the building.)

• I'm going to the college to meet my son.
(=My son is a college student and I'm meeting him there.)

• **I'm going to town** for some shopping.
       but
• The town where I live is built on a cliff.

• When I graduate from high school, I'm going to college.
       but
• The high school that I go to is an old medieval building.

| | |
|---|---|
| • **before meals** (breakfast, lunch, supper, dinner)**when we are talking about a meal in general.** ☞ | •I really **like having breakfast.** (=I like having breakfast in general.)<br>**but**<br>•I really like the breakfast that they serve in some good hotels. |
| • **before streets**☞ | • I live **on 218 Dewey street.**<br><br>• I bumped into a friend of mine **on Main street.** |
| •**before single islands**(Myconos, Santorini, etc.)☞ | **Myconos** is one of the most popular and glamourous Greek isles, well known for its non-stop party atmosphere. |
| • **before God**☞ | **God** is the creator of the universe. |

## THE INDEFINITE ARTICLE (A/AN)

| | |
|---|---|
| The Indefinite article is **used with singular countable nouns to talk about something in general** ☞ | **A boy** |
| **To talk about somebody we don't know**☞ | **A Mr. Erickson** came to see you earlier. |
| **In measurements** ☞ | He earns $3.00 **an/per hour.**<br><br>He works 30 hours **a/per week.** |
| **To refer to a person's profession** ☞ | My niece is **a dentist.**<br><br>One of my daughters is **a lawyer** and the other one is **a singer.** |
| **Before an adjective or adverb to describe a countable noun**☞ | I had **an awful day.**<br><br>You are **a very considerate person.** |

**The indefinite article a/an is not used before uncountable nouns. Some, any, much, no, a lot of, etc,** is possible with uncountable nouns:

☒ What a terrible weather.
☑ What terrible weather.

☒ I would like an advice.
☑ I would like some advice.

☒ I have a very important work to do.
☑ I have very important work to do.

☒ A knowledge of the use of the computer is necessary for this position.
☑ (Some)Knowledge of the use of the computer is necessary for this position.

## COUNTABLE NOUNS

| | |
|---|---|
| Countable nouns are both singular and plural: | **boy- boys** |
| They can be used with a/an in front of them or a number: | **a** house -**two** houses |
| Some can be used in front of countable nouns to form their plural form: | a house -**some** houses |
| The plural of most countable nouns is formed by adding an **-s** to the ending of the singular noun: | table- table**s** <br> bag -bag**s** <br> car- car**s** |
| The plural of nouns ending in **-s, -ss, -sh, -ch,** and **-x** is formed by adding **–es**: | chur**ch** - chur**ch**es <br> Bru**sh**-bru**sh**es |
| The plural of most nouns ending in **–o** is formed by adding **-es**: | carg**o**-carg**oes** <br> her**o**-her**oes** <br> mang**o**-mang**oes** <br> mosquit**o**-mosquit**oes** <br> potat**o**-potat**oes** <br> tomat**o**-tomat**oes** <br> tornad**o**-tornad**oes** <br> volcan**o**-volcan**oes** |
| If the words ending in **–o** derive from other languages an **–s** is added to form their plural: | banj**o**-banj**os** <br> concert**o**-concert**os** <br> phot**o** – phot**os** <br> pian**o**-pian**os** |

| | |
|---|---|
| Nouns that end in –**y** and are preceded by a consonant drop their - y and take –ies<br>Exception: 'monies', only which in legal documents and banking. | ba**by**- bab**ies**<br>la**dy**-lad**ies**<br>po**ny**-pon**ies** |
| If, however, the noun is **preceded by a vowel** we just add an –**s** | t**oy** - t**oys**<br>b**oy**-b**oys**<br>d**ay**-d**ay** |
| Nouns that end in- **f** or- **fe** drop the ending –f or –fe and take –**ves** to form their plural: | kni**fe**-kni**ves**<br>lea**f**-lea**ves**<br>li**fe**-li**ves**<br>scar**f**-scar**ves**<br>sel**f**-sel**ves**<br>shel**f**-shel**ves**<br>thie**f**-thie**ves**<br>wi**fe** –wi**ves** |
| There are some nouns, however, ending in **f–** or-**fe** that take-**s** to form their plural: | belie**f**-belie**fs**<br>cli**ff**-cli**ffs**<br>che**f**-che**fs**<br>chie**f**-chie**fs**<br>dwar**f**-dwar**fs**<br>handkerchie**f**-handkerchie**fs**<br>proo**f**-proo**fs**<br>roo**f**-roo**fs** |

| | |
|---|---|
| **Some nouns have** irregular plural forms: | **man - men**<br>**woman -women**<br>**mouse- mice**<br>**ox-oxen**<br>**louse- lice** |
| **Some nouns have** the same plural form as their singular form. **Some of these verbs end in- s, others describe some birds, animals and fish:** | deer, fish, salmon, headquarters, means, news, species, series, sheep, trout, etc. |
| Most **proper nouns take –s** to form their plural: | Have you met **the Robinson**s?(=the Robinson family.) |
| | |

## UNCOUNTABLE NOUNS

Uncountable nouns **do not have a plural form.** They cannot be counted and therefore **are not used with a/an, many, or a number. Some, any, much, no, a lot of etc, are possible with uncountable nouns. The verb used with uncountable nouns is singular.**

| | |
|---|---|
| Uncountable nouns are not used with numbers or a/an because they cannot be counted ☞ | Students should not **chew gum in class.** |
| For a general meaning no article is used with uncountable nouns☞ | **Chewing gum** is not allowed in the classroom. |
| For a specific meaning the article "the" can be used with uncountable nouns☞ | **I swallowed the gum** I was chewing. |
| The verb that we use with uncountable nouns is singular because uncountable nouns do not have a plural form☞ | **My hair is** short and curly.<br>**English is** my favourite subject.<br>**The furniture** in her house **is** stunning.<br>Your **money is** on the table.<br>**Meningitis** can be treated if **it is** diagnosed on time. |
| Many times we use words of quantity like **some, any, no, (a) little, much** with uncountable nouns☞ | Can I borrow **some money** from you?<br>Do you have **some/any** money?<br>Can I have **some water** please?<br>James doesn't want **any wine.**<br>I have **a little time** if you feel like chatting. |

| | |
|---|---|
| If we want to count uncountable nouns we use **a pair of scissors, pance, jeans, a glass of milk, a loaf of bread, a cup of tea, a jar of jam, a bar of chocolate, a lump of sugar, a slice of cheese** ☞ | I bought **a really nice pair of pants on sale.**<br><br>I bought **three cartons of milk.** |

List of uncountable nouns

**Substances:** oxygen, flour, bacon, beer, food, lunch, dinner, supper, coffee, tea, butter, pasta, air, grapefruit, gum, ham, milk, sugar, tea, water, wine, breakfast, alcohol.

**Most diseases:** chickenpox, flu, measles, mumps, polio, pneumonia, meningitis, rheumatism, Aids, Sars, headache, cold.

**All sports:** basketball, baseball, tennis, volleyball, hockey, cycling, canoeing, rugby, cricket.

**Nouns ending in ing:** boxing, shopping, jogging, swimming, hunting, running, sightseeing.

**Languages:** English, French, Spanish, Portuguese, Japanese, Chinese etc.

**Academic courses:** chemistry, computer science, history, geography, Ancient Greek, Modern Greek science, literature, physics, mathematics (maths),

**Abstract nouns:** greed, love, affection, peace, happiness, truth, deceit, beauty, advice, compassion, strength, applause (a round of applause), thunder, lightning.

**More uncountable nouns:** progress, money, litter, garbage, trash, rubbish, luggage, baggage, mail, news, work, hair, traffic, transport, witchcraft, sorcery, knowledge, applause.

## Countable and uncountable nouns with a difference in meaning: "company," "paper"

| uncountable | countable |
|---|---|
| Your company means the world to me. | My father owns a company that is in financial crisis. |
| Can you keep me some company tonight? | I own 50% of a company that recycles paper. |
| You are good company. | Some companies are closing due to the financial crisis. |
| Do you have some paper for the printer? | Can you get me a paper (the newspaper) when you go out. |

Note: there are some uncountable nouns that are sometimes used as countable nouns: coffee, tea, beer, wine, etc.

| Uncountable nouns ⮕ | Used as countable nouns |
|---|---|
| **Can I have some beer?** | I would like **a beer** please? |
| **I would like some coffee.** | I think I'll have **a coffee** too. |
|  | We would like **two coffees** please? |

## Singular or plural collective nouns(group nouns)

Singular or plural verbs can be used with collective nouns (group nouns).

If the members of a collective noun are acting **as a group** we use **a singular verb** and pronoun. If they are acting **as individuals** we use **a plural verb.**

Collective nouns **that can either** take a singular or a plural verb:
**(Crew, youth, army, team, committee, government, jury, majority, minority, orchestra, public, staff, team, audience, army, class, crew, crowd, team)**

The team **are ready** to begin. (the members of the team)

The team **is ready** to begin. (the team a group or unit)

**The jury have not all reached a verdict** yet. (the jury members)

**The jury has not reached a verdict** yet. (the jury as a unit)

**The jury is ready** to announce the verdict. (the jury as a unit)

## Plural collective nouns

| | |
|---|---|
| There are **some nouns** that **only take a plural verb** even if we are talking about one item: **binoculars, braces, glasses, jeans, outskirts, pants, pajamas, spectacles, stairs, scissors, shorts, statistics, tights, trousers, tweezers,** etc. | My trousers **need** to be taken in.<br><br>Where **are** the scissors? |
| **A pair of +plural nouns** can also be used with plural collective nouns that consist of two parts. The **verb** in this case can be **singular:**<br><br>**The new pair of shorts** I bought **is** fabulous.<br><br>I bought a really nice **pair of jeans** the other day.<br><br>I need **a new pair of glasses.**<br>            or<br>Can you get me **a pair of scissors,** please? | ✓I bought **some/a pair of** really nice jeans the other day.<br><br>✓I need **some/a pair** of new glasses.<br><br>✗Can you get me a scissors please?<br><br>✓Can you get me **some/a pair of** scissors please?<br><br>✓The new **shorts/pair of shorts** I bought **are** fabulous.<br><br>✓The **new pair of shorts** I bought **is** fabulous. |
| We use a plural verb to talk about nationalities when referring to groups of people (the Spanish, the British, the Welsh, the Irish, etc.) | **The British** are known for their punctuality.<br><br>**The greeks** are known to be very hospitable. |

## A few vs few
## A little vs little

**A few/few** ⮕ used with plural countable nouns.
**A little/little** ⮕ used with uncountable nouns

| | | |
|---|---|---|
| I have a few questions to ask you. | (=some) | I have some questions to ask you. |
| I have few questions to ask you. | (=not many) | I don't have many questions to ask you. |
| I have a little time for you. | (=some) | I have some time for you. |
| I have little time for you today. | (=not much) | I don't have much time for you today. |

## Some ⮕

**Some** ⮕ used with plural countable and uncountable nouns:

### in affirmative sentences

There are some people waiting for you.

There's some food on the table.

I have been up since 5 o'clock. I need some sleep.

### in interrogative sentences, requests or offers

Do we have some money for the theatre?

Would you like some coffee?

Please stay and have some tea with us.

**in interrogative sentences when we expect the answer to be positive**

You've got some time to spare, don't you?

**Derivatives: someone, somebody, something and somewhere are used in affirmative and interrogative sentences, requests or offers:**

You're hiding **something** from me, aren't you?

You know som**ething**?

Why don't we go **somewhere** and have fun tonight?

I met **someone** really nice.

**Somebody, someone, anybody, anyone are used with singular verbs:**

**Someone wants** to talk to you.

**Is anyone** here?

**Has anyone** seen my keys?

**Somebody/someone/ anybody/anyone are usually followed by they/them/their/themselves:**

Someone called. See if **they** left a message on the answering machine.

If anybody calls, tell **them** to leave a message.

No one called me while I was out, **did they?**

## Any ↻

**Any** ↻ used with plural countable and uncountable nouns:

**in negative sentences**

I don't know **any** people here.

I don't have **any** free time.

**in interrogative sentences**

Do you have **any** free time?

Have you seen **any** good films lately?

**in positive sentences after if**

If **anyone** is late for class again, they will not be allowed to take the test.

**in positive sentences to say**

You can do **anything** you like.

You can go **anywhere** you like.

You can **see anyone** you choose.

**Anyone, anybody, anything** and **anywhere** are used in **negative** and **interrogative** sentences:

Have you had **anything** to eat yet?

I haven't gone **anywhere** all weekend.

**Any, anybody, anyone** are used with singular verbs:

**Is anybody** coming with us?

I don't know **anybody** who **doesn't like** being pampered.

**Is** there **any** milk in the fridge

**Any, anyone, anybody, anything** and **anywhere** are used with negative words (hardly, scarcely, never, rarely, seldom, etc):

I **hardly go anywhere** any more.

**Hardly anybody** showed up for the lecture.

You **seldom talk to anyone** here.

The adverbs hardly, rarely, seldom, barely, scarcely, never, **have a negative meaning** and therefore, are not used with negative verbs since we cannot have two negative words in one sentence:

I **hardly go out** (=I don't go out much)

I **rarely see** him (=I don't see him often)

## No ⊃

**No** ⊃used with plural countable and uncountable nouns:

**in affirmative sentences with a negative meaning**

I **have no** money. (=I don't have any money.)

I **speak no** foreign languages. (=I don't speak any foreign languages.)

**No one, nobody, nothing** and **nowhere** are also used **in affirmative** sentences(the verb isn't negated) with a **negative meaning**:

I **know nothing** about what happened.(=I don't know anything about what happened.)

We **have been nowhere** the last five days. (=We haven't been anywhere the last five days.)

The adverbs **hardly, rarely, seldom, barely, scarcely, never,** have a **negative meaning** and therefore, **are not used with** derivatives of **'no'** since **we cannot have two negative words in one sentence.** Instead we use hardly, rarely, seldom, barely, scarcely + any, anyone, anybody, anything, anywhere):

I hardly have **any** money.(= I have very little money.)

Hardly **anyone** came to see us.(=Very few people came to see us.)

I hardly know **anybody** here.(=I know very few people here.)

I hardly **ever** go out anymore.(=I rarely go out.)

The words **nobody/ no one** are used with **affirmative singular verbs**:

**No one informs** me about anything in this house. (=I'm not informed about anything...)

**Nobody likes** to work hard, but most of us have to. (=People don't like to work hard, ...)

The lesson is boring. **Nobody pays** attention. (=The lesson is boring. The students don't pay any attention. )

**Nobody/ no one** are often **followed by they/them/their/ themselves:**

**Nobody** came, **did they?**

The party was boring. **Nobody** enjoyed **themselves**. (=the party was boring. Most of the people didn't enjoy themselves.

**Nobody is** happy with what **they have got**. (=Most people are not happy with what they've got.)

## A lot of/much/many

**A lot of** ⮕ for interrogative and affirmative sentences **with** both **countable plural nouns and uncountable nouns**

**I have a lot of money.**

**Does he have a lot of money?**

**A lot of people** attended the meeting.

**much** ⮕ for **interrogative and negative** sentences with **uncountable nouns**

**How much (money)** did you spend today?

**I don't have much money.**

**How much time** do we have left?

**many** ⮕ for **affirmative, interrogative** and **negative countable plural nouns**

Many **people** attended the lecture.

How many **cars** do you own?

I don't know many **people** here.

## Both/both of

**Both+plural nouns:**

**Both stories** were plausible.

**Both kids** are mine.

**Both of** + my/your/his/her/its/our/their/the+ **plural nouns:**

**Both of the stories** were plausible.

**Both of the kids** are mine.

## Whole/all(of)

**My/your/his/her/its/our/their/the +whole+ singular countable nouns:**

I spent **my whole life** working.

He read **the whole book** in thee hours.

**My whole week etc** was ruined.

He ate **the whole cake.**

Note : **"time" which is an uncountable noun is an exception:**

Did you spent **the whole time** talking to him?

**All(of)+ my/your/his/her/its/our/their/the +uncountable and countable singular and plural nouns:**

☑You should read **all of** the book.

☑You should read **the whole** book.

☑I spent **all(of) my life** working.

☑I spent **my whole life** working.

☑The kids drank **all(of) their milk** and ate all their food.

☑I packed **all(of) my clothes** and left.

☑He slept **all day**.

☑He slept **the whole day**.

☑He drank **all(of) his tea.**

☑He united **all(of) the family.**

☑He united **the whole family.(countable noun)**

☑He spent **all(of) his money.(uncountable noun)**

☒He spent **his whole money.(uncountable noun)**

☒The kids drank **their whole milk** and ate all their food**.(uncountable noun)**

**All of + the object pronouns**, them,us, it:

**All of them** came.
I want you to eat **all of it**.

**Irregular Vebs**

| Verb (infinitive) | Past simple | Past participle |
|---|---|---|
| **A** | | |
| arise | arose | arisen |
| awake | awoke | awoken |
| **B** | | |
| be | was/were | been |
| bear | bore | borne |
| beat | beat | beaten |
| become | became | become |
| begin | began | begun |
| bend | bent | bent |
| beset | beset | beset |
| bet | bet/betted | bet |
| bid | bid | bid |
| bind | bound | bound |
| bite | bit | bitten |
| bleed | bled | bled |
| blow | blew | blown |
| break | broke | broken |
| breed | bred | bred |
| bring | brought | brought |
| broadcast | broadcast | broadcast |
| build | built | built |
| burn | burnt/burned | burnt/burned |
| burst | burst | burst |
| buy | bought | bought |
| **C** | | |
| cast | cast | cast |
| catch | caught | caught |
| choose | chose | chosen |
| cling | clung | clung |
| come | came | come |
| cost | cost | cost |
| creep | crept | crept |

| | | |
|---|---|---|
| cut | cut | cut |
| **D** | | |
| deal | dealt | dealt |
| dig | dug | dug |
| dive | dived/dove (AmE) | dived |
| do | did | done |
| draw | drew | drawn |
| dream | dreamt /dreamed | dreamt /dreamed |
| drink | drank | drunk |
| drive | drove | driven |
| dwell | dwelt | dwelt |
| **E** | | |
| eat | ate | eaten |
| **F** | | |
| fall | fell | fallen |
| feed | fed | fed |
| feel | felt | felt |
| fight | fought | fought |
| find | found | found |
| fit | fit | fit |
| flee | fled | fled |
| fling | flung | flung |
| fly | flew | flown |
| forbid | forbade | forbidden |
| forget | forgot | forgotten |
| forego /forgo | forewent | foregone |
| forgive | forgave | forgiven |
| forsake | forsook | forsaken |
| foretell | foretold | foretold |
| freeze | froze | frozen |
| **G** | | |
| get | got | got (BrE) /gotten (AmE) |
| give | gave | given |
| go | went | gone |

| | | |
|---|---|---|
| grind | ground | ground |
| grow | grew | grown |
| **H** | | |
| hang | hung | hung |
| hang | hanged | hanged |
| have | had | had |
| hear | heard | heard |
| hide | hid | hidden |
| hit | hit | hit |
| hold | held | held |
| hurt | hurt | hurt |
| **K** | | |
| keep | kept | kept |
| kneel | knelt | knelt |
| know | knew | known |
| **L** | | |
| lay | laid | laid |
| lead | led | led |
| lean | leant /leaned | leant /leaned |
| leap | leapt /leaped | leapt /leaped |
| learn | learnt /learned | learnt /learned |
| leave | left | left |
| lend | lent | lent |
| let | let | let |
| lie | lay | lain |
| light | lit /lighted | lit /lighted |
| lose | lost | lost |
| **M** | | |
| make | made | made |
| mean | meant | meant |
| meet | met | met |
| misspell | misspelt /misspelled | misspelt /misspelled |
| mistake | mistook | mistaken |
| mow | mowed | mowed/mown |

| O | | |
|---|---|---|
| overcome | overcame | overcome |
| overdo | overdid | overdone |
| overtake | overtook | overtaken |
| overthrow | overthrew | overthrown |
| P | | |
| pay | paid | paid |
| plead | pleaded/plead | pleaded/plead |
| prove | proved | proved/proven |
| put | put | put |
| Q | | |
| quit | quit | quit |
| R | | |
| read | read | read |
| rend | rent | rent |
| rid | rid | rid |
| ride | rode | ridden |
| ring | rang | rung |
| rise | rose | risen |
| run | ran | run |
| S | | |
| saw | sawed | sawn /sawed |
| say | said | said |
| see | saw | seen |
| seek | sought | sought |
| sell | sold | sold |
| send | sent | sent |
| set | set | set |
| sew | sewed | sewn/sewed |
| shake | shook | shaken |
| shear | sheared | sheared/shorn |
| shed | shed | shed |
| shine | shone/shined | shone/shined |
| shoot | shot | shot |

| | | |
|---|---|---|
| show | showed | shown |
| shrink | shrank | shrunk |
| shut | shut | shut |
| sing | sang | sung |
| sink | sank | sunk |
| sit | sat | sat |
| sleep | slept | slept |
| slay | slew | slayed /slain |
| slide | slid | slid |
| sling | slung | slung |
| slink | slunk | slunk |
| slit | slit | slit |
| smell | smelt /smelled | smelt /smelled |
| smite | smote | smitten |
| sow | sowed | sown /sowed |
| speak | spoke | spoken |
| speed | sped /speeded | sped /speeded |
| spell | spelt /spelled | spelt /spelled |
| spend | spent | spent |
| spill | spilt /spilled | spilt /spilled |
| spin | spun | spun |
| spit | spat | spat |
| split | split | split |
| spoil | spoilt /spoiled | spoilt /spoiled |
| spread | spread | spread |
| spring | sprang | sprung |
| stand | stood | stood |
| steal | stole | stolen |
| stick | stuck | stuck |
| sting | stung | stung |
| stink | stank | stunk |
| stride | strode | stridden |
| strike | struck | struck/stricken |
| string | strung | strung |

| | | |
|---|---|---|
| strive | strove | striven |
| swear | swore | sworn |
| sweep | swept | swept |
| swell | swelled | swelled /swollen |
| swim | swam | swum |
| swing | swung | swung |
| **T** | | |
| take | took | taken |
| teach | taught | taught |
| tear | tore | torn |
| tell | told | told |
| think | thought | thought |
| thrive | thrived /throve | thrived |
| throw | threw | thrown |
| thrust | thrust | thrust |
| tread | trod | trodden |
| **U** | | |
| understand | understood | understood |
| uphold | upheld | upheld |
| upset | upset | upset |
| **W** | | |
| wake | woke /waked | woken /waked |
| wear | wore | worn |
| weave | wove /weaved | woven /weaved |
| wed | wedded /wed | wedded /wed |
| weep | wept | wept |
| wet | wet | wet |
| win | won | won |
| wind | wound | wound |
| withdraw | withdrew | withdrawn |
| withhold | withheld | withheld |
| withstand | withstood | withstood |
| wring | wrung | wrung |
| write | wrote | written |

www.ingramcontent.com/pod-product-compliance
Lightning Source LLC
Chambersburg PA
CBHW041431300426
44116CB00004B/46